Introduction to Search and Rescue

Eric H. Martin
Author, Second Edition (May 2008)

Jon Elinsky
Dan Hourihan
Editors

*Contributors to the
Second Edition*
Cole Brown, III in Maryland
Todd Brown in North Carolina
John Boburchuk, Jr. in Pennsylvania
Jon Elinsky in Pennsylvania
Mike Guzo in Virginia
George Rice in New Jersey
Susan Thrasher in Arkansas
Christopher Young in California

*Contributing Authors
To The First Edition (1999):*
Craig Bannerman – North Carolina
Steve Foster – North Carolina
Ken Hill – Nova Scotia
Rick Hood – Washington State
Susan Thrasher – Arkansas
Ed Wolff – Florida

Copyright © 1999–2008 National Association for Search and Rescue
Second Printing, 2008

Preface to the Second Edition

In the summer of 2007, NASAR Executive Director Megan Bartlett tasked Mike Guzo, ISAR/FUNSAR Program Manager, and Eric Martin to revise the Introduction to Search and Rescue (ISAR) program. The first step in this process was to identify the objectives of the ISAR program.

During the initial conversations, it was recognized that there was need for the Introduction to Search and Rescue program to prepare the initial responding resources such as police, firefighters, EMS, and CERT for missing person incidents. It was also identified that the ISAR Educational program was developed as a search and rescue awareness level training program; and, as such, should meet the NFPA 1670 Standard on Operations and Training for Technical Rescue Incidents 1999 Edition Awareness Level.

NFPA 1670 Wilderness Search and Rescue
Members of organizations at the awareness level shall be permitted to assist in support functions on a wilderness search/rescue operation but shall not be deployed into the wilderness.

Awareness-level functions at a wilderness incident shall include the following:
- Conducting a size-up of existing and potential conditions.
- Developing and implementing procedures for implementing the emergency response system for wilderness search and rescue.
- Implementing site control and scene management.
- Recognizing the general hazards associated with wilderness search and rescue incidents.
- Recognizing the type of terrain involved in wilderness search and rescue incidents.
- Recognizing the limitations of conventional emergency response skills and equipment in various wilderness environments.
- Initiating the collection and recording of information necessary to assist operational personnel in a wilderness search and rescue.
- Identifying and isolating the reporting party(s) and witnesses.

It is our hope that the Introduction to Search and Rescue program provides agencies with the knowledge and skills necessary to manage the activities during the initial phase of the search until "operational" and "technician" level SAR responders arrive.

On behalf of NASAR, I would like personally to thank the following people who contributed a significant wealth of knowledge and information, listed alphabetically: John Boburchuk, Cole Brown III, Todd Brown, Paul Burke, Jon Elinsky, Mike Guzo, Dan Hourihan, George Rice, Susan Thrasher, and Christopher Young.

Special thanks go to all of the NASAR Instructors and Evaluators who dedicate their lives to teaching search and rescue **"that others may live."**

Eric H. Martin
Ground Search Committee Chair

Preface to the Second Edition

It has been nine years since NASAR has updated and revised the ISAR textbook. This book being the second edition means that there was a lot of hard dedicated work done previously by many.

The first contributing authors were Craig Bannerman, Steve Foster, Ken Hill, Rick Hood, Susan Thrasher, and Ed Wolff.

The second was Steve Foster who served as the ISAR/FUNSAR Program Director and put a considerable amount of time and effort into the project that he was charged with in 1998 by the NASAR Board and Education Committee.

The third was Tom Millen and the members of Indiana Search and Rescue Association who hosted and conducted the pilot course which helped to ensure the textbook met the practical needs of the students.

The fourth is Don Cooper, who wrote the first book, *Search and Rescue Fundamentals*, and in 1984 urged the NASAR Board and members of the education committee to approve the development of FUNSAR as a basic search and rescue course for field personnel. Don also served as the first ISAR/FUNSAR Program Director for NASAR. He was also instrumental in the latest version of NASAR's *Fundamentals of Search and Rescue* book and worked with NASAR and Ab Taylor to ensure the future of the "Hug-A-Tree" program.

The last is Eric Martin, who took the helm of the Ground Search Education Committee and promoted the rewrite of the ISAR program in 2007. He, similar to Tom Millen, conducted a pilot course with a diverse background from EMS, firefighters, new ground searchers, and business personnel interested in search and rescue and had them use the draft material of the second edition to meet the objectives and the time frame. This pilot for the second edition was a success.

This course is a great introduction to the world of ground search and rescue for the first responder and is tailored so it can be completed in two days and would require only one test to receive both an ISAR and SARTECH™ III certificates. This course provides the first responders the ability to assess the situation and determine the necessary resources to call to ensure the timely location and rescue of a missing person.

To all of our instructors who take the time and dedication to teach the students ISAR: our hat is off to you and to our students who are devoting the time to learn how to do search and rescue so that one day they can save a life of another person and truly understand the meaning of the motto **"That Others May Live."**

Thanks,

Coleman P. Brown III

Coleman "Cole" P. Brown III
ISAR Program Manager, 2008

Introduction to Search and Rescue
Table of Contents

Chapter 1   Introduction to Search and Rescue.......................... page 8

Chapter 2   NIMS, FEMA, & Dept. of Homeland Security...... page 32

Chapter 3   Introduction to Basic Land Navigation....................page 51

Chapter 4   Search and Rescue Resource.................................. page 71

Chapter 5   Search Philosophy..page 88

Chapter 6   Clue Consciousness... page 96

Chapter 7   Search Tactics... page 105

Chapter 8   Search Operations... page 109

Chapter 9   Introduction to Lost Person Behavior.................... page 116

Chapter 10   Getting Involved.. page 123

Appendices

Appendix 1 – Incident Command System Incident Briefing 201 Form

Appendix 2 – Incident Command System Assignment List 204 Form

Appendix 3 – Incident Command System Medical Plan 206 Form

Appendix 4 – Incident Command System Check-In 211 Form

Appendix 5 – Incident Search Urgency Form

Appendix 6 – Lost Person Questionnaire Form

Appendix 7 – Incident Command System 214 Form – Unit Log

Chapter 1	Introduction to Search and Rescue

- History of Search and Rescue
  - Early Rescues of Settlers Traveling West
  - Wilderness
  - Military
  - Maritime
- Definition of Search and Rescue
- "LAST" Acronym
- Components of Search and Rescue
- National SAR Plan
- National Response Framework
- Federal, State, and Local Coordination for Search and Rescue
- Legal and Ethical Aspects of SAR, Standard of Care, Negligence
- The Six Expected Qualities of a SAR Responder

Chapter 2	NIMS, FEMA, and Department of Homeland Security

- Homeland Security Presidential Directive/HSPD-5
- Incident Command System Basics
  - Characteristics of the ICS
  - Command Staff
  - General Staff
  - Incident Facilities
- ICS and NIMS Training

Chapter 3	Introduction to Basic Land Navigation

- Importance of Orienting
- Different Types of Maps
- Compass
- Measuring Distance by Pace
- Georeferencing

Chapter 4   Search and Rescue Resources
- Introduction to the importance of using the right resource in the right place at the right time
- Human Searchers
- Trackers
- Search Management Teams
- Interviewers and Investigation
- Technical Rescue Teams
- Canine – types, advantages, and disadvantages
- Equestrian/Mounted SAR
- Alzheimer's Association, MedicAlert + Safe Return
- National Center for Missing & Exploited Children – Team Adam
- National Center for Missing Adults
- Emergent (Convergent) Volunteers
- Critical Incident Stress Management (CISM)
- Community Emergency Response Team (CERT)

Chapter 5   Search Philosophy
- Introduction to Search Theory
  - The "Crucials" of Search and Rescue
- Search Theory Terminology
  - Point Last Seen
  - Last Known Point
  - Probability of Area
  - Probability of Detection
  - Initial Planning Point
- Search Urgency
- Theoretical Search Area
- An Overview of Searcher Effectiveness

Chapter 6   Clue Consciousness
- Protecting the scene
  - The importance of not destroying clues
- Number of clues vs. number of subjects
- Clue Awareness
- Clue Orientation
- Lost Person Questionnaire
- Planning Data vs. Searching Data
- Categories of Clues
  - Physical
  - Recorded
  - Testimonial
  - Analytical
- Clue Life Span

Chapter 7	Search Tactics • An Overview of Initial Search Tactics • Direct vs Indirect Tactics

Chapter 8	Search Operations
	• Chain of actions upon arrival at the scene
	• Anatomy of the Search Effort
	• Searcher Consciousness – Responder's Attitude, Responsibilities, and Expectations
	    ○ Checking In/Out
	    ○ Proper Briefing/Debriefing
	    ○ Personal Critique

Chapter 9	Introduction to Lost-Person Behavior • Who Are We Searching for? • Why Are We Searching for Them? • Where Should We Search for Them? • When Should We Search for Them? • Search Data vs Planning Data • Factors Affecting Lost Person Behavior • Categories of Lost Persons • Preventing the Population at Risk from Becoming Lost

Chapter 10	Getting Involved
	• Laying the Foundation in Forming a SAR Team
	• Resources Available to Help Start a Team
	    ○ NASAR
	    ○ American Red Cross
	    ○ State SAR Councils

Chapter 1 –

Introduction to Search and Rescue

Chapter 1	Introduction to Search and Rescue
- History of Search and Rescue
    - Early Rescues of Settlers Traveling West
    - Wilderness
    - Military
    - Maritime
- Definition of Search and Rescue
- "LAST" Acronym
- Components of Search and Rescue
- National SAR Plan
- National Response Framework
- Federal, State, and Local Coordination for Search and Rescue
- Legal and Ethical Aspects of SAR, Standard of Care, Negligence
- The Six Expected Qualities of a SAR Responder

Upon completion of this chapter and the related course activities, the student will be able to meet the following objectives:

- Define the two distinct functions of search and rescue.
- Demonstrate the qualities of searcher attitude.
- Explain the four components of physical fitness.
- Describe the traits and characteristics of the SAR worker.
- Describe the "LAST" philosophy.
- Explain the components of SAR.
- Understand the National SAR Plan
- Describe the importance of the responsible authority
- Understand and list the six qualities of a SAR responder.

Chapter 1 – Introduction to Search and Rescue

History of Search and Rescue

Human beings, by their inherent nature, have always been willing to provide assistance and help to those in distress. This can be illustrated in the Bible when recounting the shepherd who left his herd of sheep to find the single one which was lost.

The willingness to place yourself in harm's way and possibly sacrifice one's life in an attempt to save another is just one of the many traits found in search and rescue personnel. The U.S. Air Force Pararescue and U.S. Coast Guard are two of the military agencies that have coined the motto, **"so that others may live."** For SAR personnel, this simply says it all. We do this so that others may live.

As Tim Setnicka stated in his book, *Wilderness Search and Rescue*, the ideology of self-sacrifice and assistance to others nurtured the development of any number of institutions devoted to helping and rescuing mountain travelers.

With various groups gaining interest in hiking, camping and climbing, and the desire of skiers and snowboarders craving that fresh powder in the backcountry, wilderness SAR agencies have had to create new techniques to accomplish rescue efforts. For example, the National Park Service is responsible for some of the most hazardous wilderness areas in North America and their SAR capabilities must continually be refined.

That Others May Live...

"It is my duty as a PARARESCUEMAN to save life and aid injured. I will be prepared at all times to perform my assigned duties quickly and efficiently, placing these duties before personal desires and comforts. These things I do, that others may live."

Search and Rescue has also been active in the urban setting, The New York City Urban Park Service established a wilderness search and rescue team. Although the majority of missing and overdue subjects in wilderness environments is due to the subject exceeding their personal abilities or underestimating the terrain and environment, the large percentage of missing subjects in the urban interface are dementia patients and criminal activities. In spite of the incident location, all of these subjects warrant rescue efforts if they are in jeopardy.

St. Bernard Hospice trained St. Bernard dogs to perform search and rescue by monks during the 17th century. The number of lives these dogs (and their monk trainers) saved is not known, though it is safe to say it ranges up into the hundreds. This duty was not without hazards. Documents indicate that from 1810 to 1845 avalanches cost twelve monks their lives at just this one hospice.

One monk was killed while attempting to guide a group of smugglers across a remote, untraveled path to avoid detection. Asked why smugglers and criminals were freely helped by the monks, one replied, "Our duty is to all travelers. Why they are traveling is not our concern." This lack of judgment about the motives of those in trouble largely continues in SAR teams to this day.

Tim J. Setnicka, Wilderness Search and Rescue

Search and Rescue

The first topic that needs explanation is "search and rescue," normally referred to as "SAR". This term is used to describe an incident during which we look for and evacuate a lost or overdue subject. The term SAR actually describes two distinct and separate functions:

1. **Search** – an operation using available resources to locate persons in distress.
2. **Rescue** – an operation using available resources to retrieve persons in distress, provide for their initial medical considerations, and transport them to a safe environment.

SEARCH	RESCUE
Search is to identify and locate persons who are or may become distressed or injured and are unable to return to a place of safety on their own.	Rescue is to access, stabilize, and evacuate distressed or injured persons, by whatever means necessary, to ensure their timely transfer to an appropriate care facility or to a familiar environment.

Searcher Attitude

Why do you want to do search and rescue? There are numerous answers to this fundamental question. However, since there is little or no financial compensation, most people do search and rescue because of an inherent motivation to help others in need. The backbone of every search effort is primarily volunteers and involves extremely demanding work. The SAR worker spends much more time training than in actual response time. SAR responders can't schedule assignments, so their personal lives may be sacrificed at times. Their families are asked to develop a significant level of patience and understanding out of respect for the SAR responder's character, which is truly in their blood. "So that others may live" is more than a phrase. It is a searcher's way of life.

A person should not get involved in SAR if they are looking for personal gain, fame or fortune. In truth, SAR is difficult work, requiring long hours, physically demanding activities, with emotional highs and lows and usually some financial sacrifice. The SAR individual needs to prepare both physically and mentally.

The searcher should focus on preparing themselves physically by focusing on four components of total overall fitness **[S.A.F.E.]**:

Strength – the ability to exert force on physical objects using muscles. Strength can be divided into two categories Short-term endurance and long-term endurance.

Agility – the ability to successfully change the body's direction efficiently, using a combination of coordination, speed, and strength.

Flexibility – the ability to adapt the body to different positions under different circumstances. Stretching is essential prior to starting physical activities; it will also reduce musculoskeletal injuries.

Endurance – is different from other forms of physical stress in that fatigue of the muscle and cardiovascular system do not force the effort to end. The need for sleep, build-up of non-recyclable body waste chemicals, depletion of energy stores, psychological failure, or achieving the goal will bring the effort to an end.

Attributes of mental fitness include:

- Be thorough
- Be confident and willing to learn
- Be conscientious
- Be assertive
- Be a team player
- Be humble and know your limitations

Qualities of the SAR Individual
It is important that SAR workers understand exactly what is expected by managers and leaders. As a helpful tool to remember these key guidelines, the acronym "PHACKS" was devised to convey these expectations. SAR workers should use these guidelines when attempting to exhibit the qualities necessary to become a team player in the field.

Proficient – Performing with expert correctness and competency. Being adept and proficient at what you do.

Humble – Being unpretentious, modest and identifying one's shortcomings.

Able – Capable of performing, both physically and mentally.

Competent – The ability to perform a task.

Knowledgeable – Familiarity, awareness, or understanding gained through formal study and experience.

Solicitous – Full of polite concern for the well-being of others; marked by or given to anxious care and often hovering attentiveness.

The science of search and rescue has evolved substantially over the course of recent decades and, with this process, a number of core elements have been affirmed repeatedly. The most important element is that early recognition and assessment of the search incident and rapid activation of trained search agencies and organizations is crucial in influencing the survivability of the subject.

All responders, from the incident managers and searchers to the individuals delivering the port-a-johns, are working towards locating and successfully rescuing the subject. The cohesiveness of the team can lead to a smoother response, incident assessment, and transition of strategic plans to tactical assignments.

Each searcher should focus his/her energies into a positive, "can-do," safe attitude. Being proficient with knowledge and skills will provide them with a level of confidence, which will spread to other rescuers.

The "LAST" Philosophy
All SAR operations proceed through four phases, known as the four Core Elements listed by Tim Setnicka in his book, *Wilderness Search and Rescue*. The "LAST" acronym provides the searcher with a template that addresses the four different phases of the SAR effort. The "LAST" acronym stands for **L**ocate, **A**ccess, **S**tabilize, and **T**ransport. Each phase is described below.

Locate represents the act of searching for and finding the subject that is lost, misplaced or injured and unable to return to a place of safety on their own. This requires that responders have the skills needed to go out and find overdue or lost subjects as well as survive and function in that same environment so as not to become a liability or part of the problem. This is usually the longest and most difficult phase of the SAR operation. Finding a person in an urban, suburban or wilderness environment all pose certain challenges. The "Locate" phase of the response should prioritize its efforts on distinguishing relevant clues in order to locate the subject.

Access represents the phase of gaining a safe approach once the subject has been located. There have been many occasions in which the location of the subject has been established; however, gaining access to them may have been delayed due to various external factors. The subject may signal using a flare, a mirror, smoke or some other method. But, due to terrain characteristics, it may take hours or days for a rescue team to hike to the subject. Priority during this phase should be focused on rescuer safety. The searchers should not develop tunnel vision when they locate the subject and, in their haste to get to the subject, jeopardize their own personal safety.

Stabilize represents the phase in which rescuers focus their efforts on maintaining the physical and mental well-being of the subject until he/she can be transferred to a safe environment. This may include providing medical attention such as basic first aid or advanced life support. It may just involve emotional support and food and water so that they may be able to walk-out of the environment with their own abilities under the supervision of the rescuers. In most parts of the United States, search managers have a medically trained member on each crew or task assignment. Regardless of medical training, we need to be able to recognize the subject's requirements and have the ability to request the additional resources required for the his/her needs.

Transport is the phase which requires moving the patient to an appropriate care facility (emergency room or trauma center) or to a safe and/or known location. There are many types of transportation available ranging from walking the subject out to carrying a victim out in a litter, to ATVs, ambulances and/or helicopters. It could include transporting the victim in a litter and hoisting to a hovering helicopter, to short-hauling via a helicopter, to a ground transport unit. The rescuer will need to understand the requirements to safely and efficiently transport the patient to safety.

Each of the above phases occur on a time line. The Locate Phase is the function of Search while the Access, Stabilize, and Transport Phases are the functions of Rescue. During this entire time line, there is a crucial function that needs to occur – the follow-up investigation – from the initial call for help through the post-interview with the victim. That investigation may be, and preferably is, conducted by law enforcement.

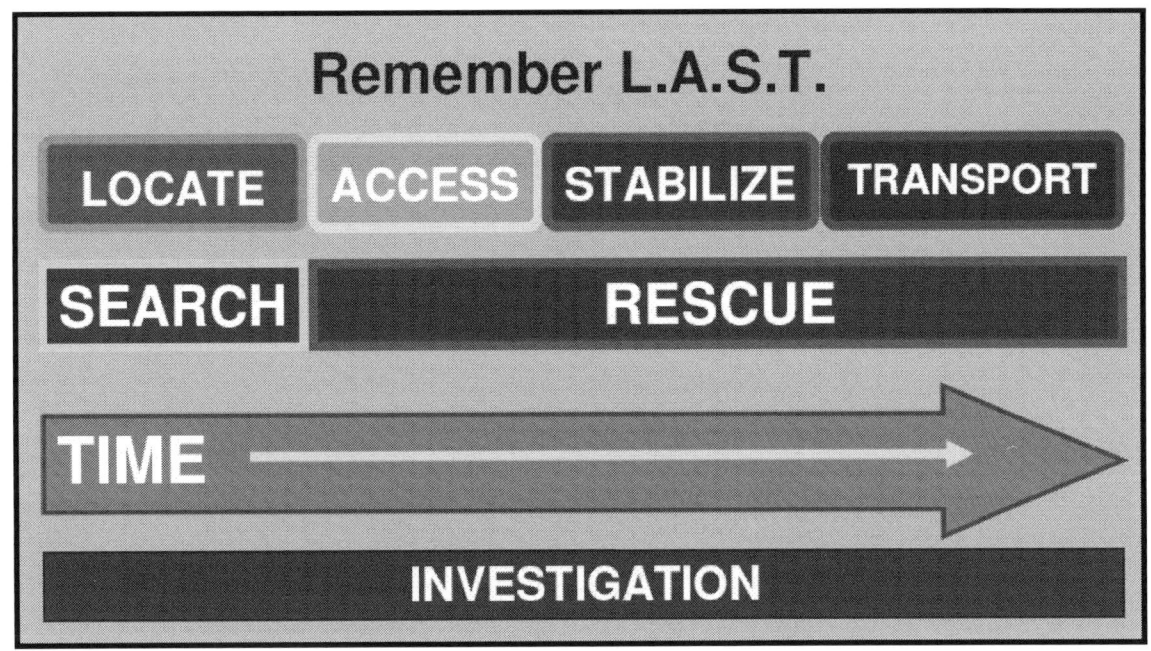

Components of Search and Rescue

The awareness level and support personnel should understand that there is more involved in the search effort than just entering the woods or streets and searching for the missing subject. There should be some preplanning efforts done by others long before anyone ever enters the woods or steps on the concrete to begin the search effort. There are many questions to answer, including but not limited to: How are you to be notified if there is a search for a missing subject? What will be the minimum standards of training? What types of maps will your team use? How long can your team stay onsite?

In order to begin the process of answering some of these questions, one must understand the components of search and rescue. The components of search and rescue are dynamic and fluid. They should assist the SAR team with justifying when and why operational standards should be changed or updated. The components of search and rescue occur in chronological order and several of the components overlap during the search and rescue event and can be portrayed in circular sequence.

These components include:
1. Preplanning
2. Notification
    a. Team Notification
    b. Team Member Notification
3. Planning and Strategy
4. Operations and Tactics
5. Suspension
    a. Demobilization
6. Critique, After Action Report, Lessons Learned Review and/or Modify Training
    a. Modification of Preplan

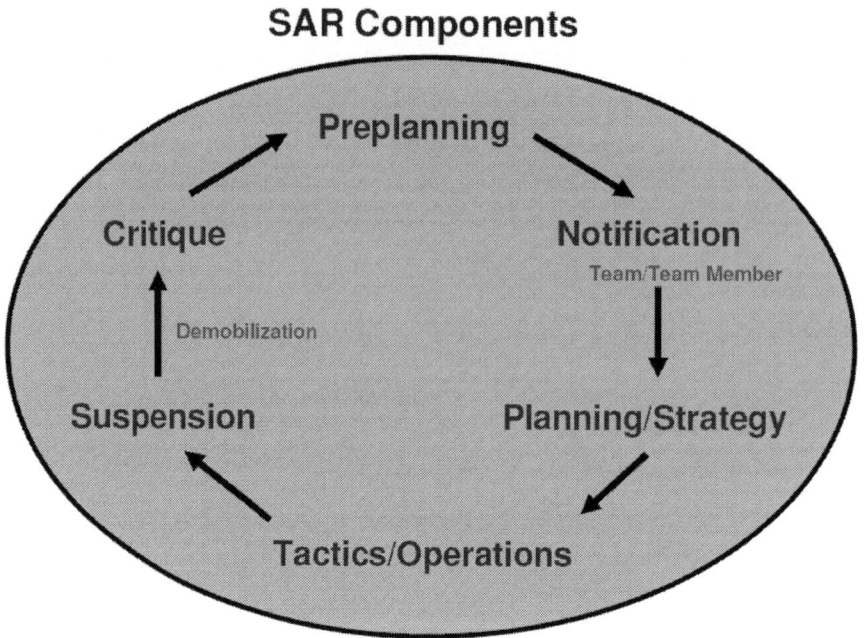

SAR Components

Preplanning

Preplanning is the process of preparing for a SAR response ahead of time. There are two aspects of the preplanning phase: 1) the team, and 2) the team member.

There are many questions that should be answered prior to actually responding to a search incident. Proper preplanning is essential in order to be prepared for the response. There needs to be an understanding of the vulnerabilities and potential problems that can be foreseen. Some of the following questions should be addressed in the preplanning phase:

- What type of missing person searches have we had in our area in the past?
- What type of searches do we foresee in the future?
- What is the local terrain and environment?
- What level of training will be required?
- What standards and credentialing will be required?
- What type of equipment will be required?
- What types of maps will be used?
- What will the area of response consist of?
- What types of packs will the team use?
- How often will training take place?
- What type of communication will be utilized?
- How long can the team operate at an incident?
- What services will the team offer?
- What services will the team not offer?
- Will the team offer Preventative Search and Rescue training programs like "Hug-A-Tree"?

- Do we need to establish a "Memorandum of Understanding" with Responsible Authorities?
- Do we need insurance? (Professional liability, vehicle, worker's compensation, etc.)
- Does the team have written policies and procedures?
- What are the policies for communicating to the media and family?

It is crucial for the team members to begin to develop a conscious attitude to become physically and mentally prepared for the search incident. Team members should maintain a physical exercise program in order to achieve the endurance needed for foot travel. Members should also attend formal training in order to develop confidence when assigned a task.

Primarily, these events require proper preplanning so that the highest efficiency can be achieved in the shortest time in a safe manner.

Preplanning is preparing the team, the teammates, and you for unpredictable events in the future and allows you to envision various situations in advance. This process is proactive versus reactive.

The "Hug-A-Tree" program is a prime example of proactive community outreach to demonstrate to the youth and others what to do if they should become lost.

Hug-A-Tree Program
On a Saturday in February 1981, three brothers were together on Palomar Mountain, 60 miles northeast of San Diego. They were walking on a popular nature trail a half-mile from the camp where their parents were preparing lunch. Two of the brothers believed that the nine-year-old was racing them back to camp, but Jimmy Beveridge never arrived.

The family spent one hour searching on their own before contacting a Park Ranger who in turn contacted the Sheriff's Office. By late afternoon, the sheriff's helicopter arrived, Sheriff's Reserve Search and Rescue personnel were beginning to assemble, and members of the San Diego Mountain Rescue Team arrived. The official search had begun and quickly escalated as operations continued into the night.

As is often the case in February in Southern California, the weather was unpredictable. Saturday had dawned beautifully clear. It was warm in the sun and cool enough for a jacket in the shade. There were still patches of snow in the areas the sun didn't reach. As nightfall approached, clouds and fog moved in and the temperature steadily dropped.

By Monday it was raining almost continuously and fog continued to shroud the mountain top. The helicopters could fly only when the cloud ceiling retreated, which was rare on this day. The wind and rain had neutralized Jimmy's scent, so tracking dogs were of no use. The only hope was to systematically search the entire area, and pray for a sign of the boy.

> Tuesday morning the weather broke and the sun came out. There were about 400 searchers on the scene, including 200 marines. That afternoon the boy's jacket and one shoe were recovered and his direction of travel was finally established. Wednesday morning Jimmy's body was found, curled up next to a tree in a ravine about two miles from the campground. He had died from hypothermia.
>
> The tragedy gnawed at Ab Taylor, a professional tracker for the U.S. Border Patrol, and Tom Jacobs, a freelance photographer. Both had been members of the search teams that worked tirelessly to find Jimmy. It was the first time in Mr. Taylor's 31 years as a tracker that he had failed to find a missing child alive, and the experience prompted him to enlist Tom Jacob's collaboration in establishing Project Hug-A-Tree – a program aimed at teaching youngsters what to do if they're lost.

Notification
Notification is separated into two categories:
1. Notification of the search assignment to the search team.
2. Notification of the search assignment to the team member.

Notification by the team that a search incident is beginning is ultimately the responsibility of the search team. The search team is responsible for establishing relationships with law enforcement agencies prior to the search incident as part of the preplan.

The team member contacting the responsible authority should gather some basic information when initially making contact. This usually occurs by phone or in person. The information is also known as "searching and planning data" and includes the following:

- The subject(s) name
- Physical description including age, weight, height, hair color, eye color
- Where was the subject planning to go and why?
- How long has the subject been missing?
- Where was the subject last seen or known to have been and who can verify it?
- Did the subject take any supplies or equipment?
- Does the subject have any survival skills or experience?
- Who to contact for more information and/or if the subject is found?
- Photograph of the subject (as recent as possible)
- Subject's shoe description (if possible)
- Where to respond to (i.e., the command post or staging area)
- Special conditions or problems expected
- What special equipment or resources are needed?
- Cancellation contact information

It is vital that this basic information since it should be passed on to the team members responding to the search incident. Members should start the search process as they are driving to the scene since the subject may be traveling away from the scene thus creating a possibility of crossing paths. It also gives the team member an opportunity to get familiar with the area.

Planning and Strategy
The Planning phase provides the response team with an on-scene operational plan. This phase establishes an overhead team or search manager that will collect and evaluate specific details of the incident. This phase establishes objectives that develop into an on-scene operational plan leading to various tactics which can be used to search and ultimately rescue the missing person.

A plan is a series of actions (strategies) thought out with a particular goal. During a missing person search and rescue incident, the goal is "Success Fast" and the objective is to efficiently find the missing person fast, and unharmed.

Ideally, your plan tells you the specific tactics that searchers will take to implement the strategy. Confinement, hasty searching, and investigations are strategies. Road and trail blocks are tactics for the strategy of confinement. Checking likely spots, calling the missing persons name, and rapidly searching all the trails and roads are tactics for the strategy of hasty searching. The strategy can be both short-term and long-term. Ultimately the strategy leads us to the goal, which is to find the missing person fast and unharmed.

The terms *tactics* and *strategy* are often confused: a *tactic* is an action used to achieve an objective, while *strategy* is the overall plan or series of actions, which may involve complex patterns of individual tactics.

Originally confined to military matters, the word tactic has become commonly used in many different fields.

> *"Do not repeat the tactics which have gained you one victory, but let your methods be regulated by the infinite variety of circumstances."* – Sun Tzu

The planning phase is ongoing and dynamic as new situational information is received and interpreted. New plans and strategies are developed and resources are tasked accordingly.

The Planning Section Chief has the responsibility to develop the strategy and overall plan that will be carried out by operations and the Operations Section Chief.

Operations and Tactics
Once the plan and strategies are developed, we now need to implement the plan. This is done during the operational phase, where resources carry out various tactics. The operation is the component of the search effort in which the search personnel and resources are actually assigned to tasks.

Tactics are the actions resources use to find a direction of travel, confine the search area or attract a subject and the tactical elements may include, but are not limited to, the following:

- Which SAR resources are best suited to accomplish the planned strategy?
- Where will the SAR resource search within the search area?
- When will SAR resources begin the search?
- How will the SAR resource search?

There are numerous types of tactical resources within search and rescue (examples are ground searchers, K9's, equestrian/mounted searchers, trackers, aviation [helicopter or planes], investigators, etc.) It is essential that the most effective and efficient tactics are used in order to achieve the highest possibility of overall success. **Use the right tool for the right job at the right time.**

It is also beneficial to consider using multiple resources simultaneously. For example, have an overhead search management team establish subject profiles, median distance traveled, and deploy a Hasty Team to reconnoiter possible routes of travel. At the same time the tracking/trailing canines are searching the last known point of contact. Then plan to use a tracker to sign-cut the last known point as an ideal way to get resources started and attain the best results.

The Operations Section Chief is designated to assign the resources appropriate for the tactic.

It is ultimately the responsibility of the Incident Commander to assure that there is a plan with various strategies and that operations use the most appropriate tactic for each resource being assigned.

Suspension
Ultimately, the search will have to be suspended; we hope that it is because the subject has been safely located. Unfortunately subjects are also found deceased.

However, in the event that the subject is not located, the decision to suspend the search effort must be considered as the search effort continues over the course of time. The following topics indicate when a search might need to be suspended:

- Lack of clues within the search area
- Expenditure of all SAR resources
- External influences
- Financial resources needed to continue search efforts

In certain cases we may suspend active searching until further investigation identifies additional leads or clues, or until additional resources are obtained.

No matter why the search is suspended, a plan should be developed to demobilize enroute and on-scene resources. The process of demobilization is to ensure equipment and personnel are returned to "Ready Status" and to ensure the resource return home safely. "Ready Status" means returning the equipment, charging radio batteries, refueling, cleaning, and replacing used equipment. Ready Status of personnel may include signing out of personnel, ensuring they have adequate sleep, water and food prior to leaving, and checking that they return home safely. Demobilization plans in some incidents may require a written plan, but in many incidents it is only verbal.

Critique and After-Action Report
The critique is considered the last phase. However, since the cycle is continuous, the critique is an essential phase of the components of Search and Rescue because it becomes the first step of updating the preplan for the next mission. It will become the basis for the evolution of any team's pre-plan and guidelines. As the team becomes more operationally experienced, it should incorporate those experiences into what worked, and just as important, what needs to be improved. The critique provides an opportunity for everyone involved at the incident to get a more complete understanding of what was done, why it was done a particular way, and what was the outcome. Items from the critique may drive changes in training, equipment, material, and procedures.

The critiques assist the team leaders in preparing their subordinates for leadership roles at future incidents.

The National SAR Plan

The National Search and Rescue Plan (NSP) was developed primarily to provide guidance to signatory federal agencies (agencies who participate in the plan) for coordinating civil SAR services to meet domestic needs and international commitments.

Guidance for implementing the NSP is provided in the *International Aeronautical and Maritime Search and Rescue Manual* (IAMSAR), the *National Search and Rescue Supplement* (NSS), and other relevant directives or addendums of the plan participants.

The National SAR Committee (NSARC) is responsible for coordinating and improving federal involvement in civil search and rescue for the aeronautical, maritime, and land communities within the United States.

NSARC Member Agencies

Many U.S. states have chosen to retain established SAR responsibilities within their boundaries for incidents primarily local or intrastate in character. In such cases, agreements have been made between SAR coordinator(s) and relevant state organizations. For land SAR, the federal SAR Coordinator is the U.S. Air Force, which maintains a rescue coordination center (RCC) known as the Air Force Rescue Coordination Center (AFRCC) at Tyndall Air Force Base in Florida. The relevant state organizations vary from state to state, but agreements exist between each state and the AFRCC.

Photograph courtesy of Jim Bartlett

The National Response Framework (NRF)

The *National Response Framework* (NRF) presents the guiding principles that enable all response partners to prepare for and provide a unified national response to disasters and emergencies. It establishes a comprehensive, national, all-hazards approach to domestic incident response. The *National Response Plan* was replaced by the *National Response Framework* effective March 22, 2008.

The *National Response Framework* defines the principles, roles, and structures that organize how we respond as a nation. The *National Response Framework*:

- Describes how communities, tribes, states, the federal government, private-sectors, and nongovernmental partners work together to coordinate national response;
- Describes specific authorities and best practices for managing incidents; and
- Builds upon the National Incident Management System (NIMS), which provides a consistent template for managing incidents.

In addition, it describes special circumstances where the federal government exercises a larger role, including incidents where federal interests are involved and catastrophic incidents where a state would require significant support. It lays the groundwork for first responders, decision-makers and supporting entities to provide a unified national response.

> The *NRF* is built on the following five principles:
> - Engaged partnerships
> - Tiered response
> - Scalable, flexible and adaptable operational capabilities
> - Unity of effort through unified command
> - Readiness to act

In addition to releasing the *NRF* base document, the Emergency Support Function Annexes and Support Annexes are available on-line at the NRF Resource Center (www.fema.gov/nrf). The annexes are a total of 23 individual documents designed to provide concept of operations, procedures and structures for achieving response directives for all partners in fulfilling their roles under the *NRF*.

One of these Emergency Support Functions is *ESF #9 – Search and Rescue* (www.fema.gov/pdf/emergency/usr/mod1_u2.pdf) and it is an all-hazards search and rescue response document for:

- Structural Collapse (Urban) Search and Rescue (US&R)
- Waterborne Search and Rescue
- Inland/Wilderness Search and Rescue
- Aeronautical Search and Rescue

SAR services include the performance of distress monitoring, communications, location of distressed personnel, coordination, and execution of rescue operations including extrication or evacuation along with the provisioning of medical assistance and civilian services through the use of public and private resources to assist persons and property in potential or actual distress.

In April 2008 The National Search and Rescue Committee (NSARC) developed the *Catastrophic Incident Search and Rescue (CIS) Addendum* to the *National Search and Rescue Manual* (NSM). The purpose of the *CIS* is to:

- Provide a concise description of federal governments civil SAR response to catastrophic incidents;
- Guide federal authorities involved in a CIS response; and
- Inform States on what to expect of federal SAR responders during catastrophic incidents

Federal, State, and Local Coordination for Search and Rescue

United States Air Force

The AFRCC realigned under 1st Air Force (AFNORTH) in April 2006, to consolidate Air Force support to civilian agencies under a single air component commander.

Previously located at Langley AFB, Virginia, the AFRCC is now consolidated with the 601st Air Operations Center, giving it greater ability to leverage Air Force air and space capabilities that can be applied to continental U.S. search and rescue.

The AFRCC serves as the single agency responsible for coordinating inland federal SAR activities in the 48 contiguous United States, Mexico and Canada.

Serving as a communication hub during ongoing search and rescue missions, the AFRCC provides coordination and assistance to on-scene commanders, mission coordinators, and incident commanders in order to recover the mission's objective in the safest and most effective manner possible. This 24/7 center uses state-of-the-art technology, including network satellites for monitoring emergency locator transmitter signals to help reduce the critical time required to locate and recover people in distress.

They maintain a close working relationship and coordination with the Federal Aviation Administration and the Civil Air Patrol (CAP).

The AFRCC maintains a Memorandum of Agreement (MOA) between 1st Air Force (AFNORTH) and state governors and a Memorandum of Understanding (MOU) between the AFRCC and state SAR Agencies. This outlines how civil search and rescue will be conducted for ground (missing persons) and aeronautical (missing aircraft) subjects.

Since the center opened in May 1974, AFRCC missions have resulted in more than 13,938 lives saved.

Federal Aviation Administration

The Federal Aviation Administration (FAA) is responsible for providing search information for missing and downed aircraft. This is accomplished through the Flight Services organization. One of Flight Service's most important responsibilities is in the area of search and rescue. Flight Service Stations (FSS) are valuable resources in initiating the chain of events when an aircraft becomes overdue. For aircraft emergencies, distress, and urgency, information will be given to the appropriate Rescue Coordination Center (RCC) through a Flight Service Station or an en-route FAA Center. A filed flight plan is the most timely and effective indicator that an aircraft is overdue. Flight plan information is invaluable to SAR resources in planning and executing search efforts.

Civil Air Patrol

The Civil Air Patrol (CAP) is the civilian auxiliary of the U.S. Air Force and is organized within the military structure. Civil Air Patrol was conceived in the late 1930s by legendary New Jersey aviation advocate Gill Robb Wilson, who foresaw aviation's role in war and general aviation's potential to supplement America's military operations. With the help of New York Mayor Fiorello La Guardia, the new Civil Air Patrol was established on December 1, 1941, just days before the Japanese attacked Pearl Harbor.

Perhaps best known for its search and rescue efforts, CAP now flies more than 85% of all federal inland search and rescue missions directed by the Air Force Rescue Coordination Center. The Civil Air Patrol is a valuable local resource in most parts of the country. They are a private nonprofit, 501(c)(3) corporation, an auxiliary of the U.S. Air Force (volunteers), are in eight geographic regions with 52 wings and headquartered at Maxwell Air Force Base, Alabama. CAP has three congressionally mandated missions:

- Aerospace Education and Safety
- Cadet Program
- Emergency Services

They have over 56,000 members, 850 vehicles, and 550 airplanes throughout the United States.

U.S. Coast Guard

The U.S. Coast Guard (USCG) is responsible for all search and rescue activities on any body of navigable water in the United States.

Search and Rescue (SAR) is one of the Coast Guard's oldest missions. Minimizing the loss of life, injury, property damage or loss by rendering aid to persons in distress and property in the maritime environment has always been a Coast Guard priority. Coast Guard SAR response involves multi-mission stations, cutters, aircraft, and boats linked by communications networks. The *National SAR Plan* divides the U.S. area of SAR responsibility into internationally recognized inland and maritime SAR regions. The Coast Guard is the Maritime SAR Coordinator. This response network has evolved into the state-of-the-art model for search and rescue in the world.

The U.S. Coast Guard is also responsible for the National Distress and Response System (NDRS) Coverage: NDRS is the primary distress alerting and SAR command, control and communications (C3) system for U.S. coastal waters (Sea Area A-1, which extends from the territorial baseline out to 20 nautical miles).

The benchmarks the U.S. Coast Guard has established for itself are:

- **Save at least 93% of those people whose lives are in distress.**
- Prevent the loss of at least **80% of the property** that is at risk of destruction.

The USCG also serves as the secretariat for the National Search and Rescue Committee (NSARC).

State Search and Rescue Authorities

State responsibility is generally in the form of coordination and legislation. The state identifies responsibility for SAR and may determine how the local authority coordinates and activates resources. Many states also establish standards for search and rescue teams and their members. The state is also the point of contact for activation of resources available from the federal government. The state's responsibility is outlined in the Memorandum of Agreement (MOA) and Memorandum of Understanding (MOU) as described earlier under the AFRCC for civil search and rescue for ground (missing persons) and aeronautical (missing aircraft) searches. Some states will direct response and coordination while there are other states that do not provide any direct response on a search, but rather make their resources available if a local agency needs assistance and help beyond their means. This may be very beneficial from a financial standpoint as many times when the state is asked to become involved in a search, they may assume some or all of the cost. As a search and rescue responder you should understand and know if your state has a State SAR Coordinator, a State SAR Plan, and/or legislation regarding search and rescue.

Local SAR Authority / Responsible Authority

Local search and rescue teams are the backbone of all search and rescue missions in the United States. Without local SAR teams there would not be trained SAR resources for which a town, county, or province could call upon when someone is lost and in need of assistance. This SAR response by and large comes from volunteer organizations that function under the jurisdiction of a local or state governmental agency responsible for search and rescue response and coordination.

Similar to other volunteer public safety agencies such as fire departments and emergency medical services, the monetary value that volunteer SAR organizations save municipalities during these potential multi-operational incidents are immeasurable.

Generally, the responsibility of SAR at the local level is delegated to either 1) law enforcement, or 2) emergency management. As a general rule the local law enforcement agency or county sheriff's department, especially in the western portions of the United States are responsible for SAR activities. In the eastern portion of the U.S. the responsibility tends to be divided between the local law enforcement and the local emergency management agency.

Although many search teams may be attached to, or act as a component of, the agency of the jurisdiction, they are usually staffed mostly if not completely by volunteers.

The Responsible Authority is defined as the government agency or agencies who have legal responsibility for finding missing persons and has jurisdiction over the area where the person becomes missing.

Due to the potential criminal nature of missing person search and rescue operations, the responsible authority is the law enforcement agency of that jurisdiction. The SAR incident could end up as a homicide, suicide, or abduction.

> **Remember:**
> As long as the **Classical Mystery** is involved, a law enforcement agency should be the responsible authority and should remain in charge to maintain the continuity of the chain of evidence.

Search and Rescue Teams

Search and rescue teams can be associated with fire departments, rescue squads, sheriff's reserve units, emergency management agencies, and as totally independent, non-profit, non-governmental organizations.

Legal and Ethical Aspects of SAR

Some legal issues applicable to the provision of emergency care are so important that they are considered essential knowledge for all SAR personnel. Although a comprehensive overview of legal issues related to SAR cannot be provided here, some of the most important issues related to emergency services personnel will be reviewed in the context of search and rescue. SAR organizations and personnel have a responsibility to seek competent legal council when questions arise.

Standard of Care
All rescue personnel are required by law to act or behave toward others in a certain way regardless of the activity involved. Depending on the situation, one may have a duty to either act or not act. How one acts or behaves is called a standard of care.

Several factors influence the standard of care and therefore the appropriateness of one's conduct. Local customs, statutes, ordinances, regulations, and professional and institutional standards all have a bearing on the measure of one's actions. SAR personnel should research their local standards and governances.

Negligence
The outcome of even the best run SAR incident is always unpredictable. Unfortunately, the subject of a SAR incident can allege that the care rendered, or the rescue performed, was improper, inadequate, or negligent. Negligence is the failure to provide the same care someone with similar training and in a similar situation would provide.

In order to determine negligence, the following four factors must be present:

- Duty – The rescuer had a duty to act reasonably within his or her training.
- Breach of Duty – The rescuer failed to perform that duty and did not act within the accepted and reasonable standard of care.
- Damages – The subject was injured or harmed.
- Causes – The rescuer's failure was the cause of the subject's injury or loss.

The heavy burden to prove these four requirements is a strong deterrent against frivolous and unjustified lawsuits.

Six Expected Traits and Characteristics of a SAR Responder

A searcher should be: Professional, Competent, Prepared, Focused, Trained, Caring

Professional
The searcher should present and prepare as any professional would. There should always be an attitude of confidence and dedication to the job at hand. A searcher needs to approach each function as if they were being evaluated for a promotion and do the absolute best that their ability and training allows.

Competent
Competence is defined as "having requisite or adequate abilities or qualities." This means that when a searcher responds to a search, that they know what is expected of them and are ready to perform to that level. Searchers become competent through experience, training, testing and performing to a standard. One way to increase a search manager's confidence in a searcher's competence is for the searcher to become certified.

Prepared
The searcher should be mentally and physically prepared to search. This includes having the proper attitude, physical fitness level, and equipment and clothing to be able to get the job done. It is up to each searcher to provide this preparedness and know that if they are not prepared to search, they must not respond.

Focused
A searcher must always be ready to listen, look, and observe the world around them. This is required when being briefed about the search, while searching, and throughout the entire incident. Search is a response built around details, some very small. A searcher must always be focused on what is being said to them, what they are saying to others, and what they see and observe when they are searching. They must not become distracted from the search.

Trained
No matter how dedicated or competent a person appears, we have learned through years of research and experience that we cannot allow ourselves to use untrained resources on a search. This has a devastating effect on the incident. Only trained persons can be relied on to search without destroying and/or missing clues that hold the key to finding the missing subject. Every searcher must seek out courses and continue to learn as long as they continue to respond to searches. Searchers should make sure that the agencies responsible for SAR in their jurisdiction are aware of the level of training teams and individual resources have.

Caring
The searcher should also have a set purpose in mind when responding. This purpose should be to find the missing subject, and this should be the reason that the searcher is there. This is a concept reinforced by the motto, ***"so that others may live"*** used by search and rescue organizations worldwide. The searcher should have the attitude that the missing subject is a member of their family that they love and care about. This attitude must be maintained even if there are rumors and unconfirmed opinions about the victim.

Chapter 1 Review Questions

1. What is the definition of search?

   _____

   _____

2. What is the definition of rescue?

   _____

   _____

3. List the components of SAR:

   a) _____

   b) _____

   c) _____

   d) _____

   e) _____

   f) _____

4. What is the definition of a "tactic"?

   _____

   _____

5. Describe the two stages of "notification" as described in the components of SAR:

   _____

   _____

6. Define four core elements of the "LAST" acronym:

   _____

   _____

   _____

   _____

7. Preplanning is necessary because it provides:

_____
_____
_____
_____

8. What factors would require the suspension of a search?

_____
_____
_____
_____

9. What is the AFRCC and what is its function?

_____
_____

10. What are the six expected qualities of a SAR responder?

   a) _____
   b) _____
   c) _____
   d) _____
   e) _____
   f) _____

11. What are the benefits of holding a critique?

_____
_____
_____
_____

12. List four components of overall fitness:

    a) _____
    b) _____
    c) _____
    d) _____

13. List four attributes of mental fitness:

    a) _____
    b) _____
    c) _____
    d) _____

14. Describe why law enforcement should be the responsible agency for a SAR event?

    _____
    _____
    _____
    _____

15. What are the three congressional mandates of the Civil Air Patrol?

    a) _____
    b) _____
    c) _____

Chapter 2 –

NIMS, FEMA, and Department of Homeland Security

Chapter 2 NIMS, FEMA, and Department of Homeland Security
- Homeland Security Presidential Directive/HSPD-5
- Incident Command System Basics
  - Characteristics of the ICS
  - Command Staff
  - General Staff
  - Incident Facilities
- ICS and NIMS Training

Upon completion of this chapter and the related course activities, the student will be able to meet the following objectives:

- Identify the four characteristics of an Incident Command System.
- Describe the five functional areas of the Incident Command System.
- Describe the general responsibilities of the Command and General Staff.
- Explain the functions of the following Incident Facilities:
  a) Incident Command Post
  b) Staging Area
  c) Incident Base
  d) Helibase
  e) Helispot
- Understand the Chain of Command.
- Understand Unity of Command.
- Understand Span of Control.

Chapter 2 – NIMS, FEMA & Department of Homeland Security

This chapter is an introduction into the world of search management. Search and Rescue missions, like any other emergency, can become chaotic very quickly. It is essential that the searcher understand and work within the established management system, no matter what their rank is, to ensure as much order as possible.

Search and Rescue incident management shares similar roots with other emergency disciplines. Those roots are with an all-risk-incident management system developed by a task force of fire, EMS, law enforcement, emergency management, and wildland fire professionals after a catastrophic series of California wildfires in the 1970s. That committee, later known as FIRESCOPE (Firefighting Resources of California Organized for Potential Emergencies), developed the '*Incident Command System (ICS)*' model that has been adopted as part of what today is called the National Incident Management System (NIMS).

Since the late 1970s, ICS had primarily been used in wildfire applications. Slowly, over the years, it proved effective and was adopted sparingly for use in various first-response disciplines. Unfortunately, many responders adopted it and made sometimes subtle modifications to fit their needs. Soon, there were ICS models with slight modifications for Fire, Wildland Fire, Law Enforcement, Public Works, and even Wilderness Search and Rescue. These subtle changes affected their response and resulted in conflicts and poor communications during emergencies.

Those catastrophic events that exceeded local, state, and federal resources and challenged the different management systems opened yet another chapter for responders at all levels. The Federal Emergency Management Agency (FEMA) has been in existence since 1979, and began development of an Integrated Emergency Management System with an all-hazards approach that included "direction, control and warning systems which are common to the full range of emergencies from small isolated events to the ultimate emergency – war." Since then, FEMA's mission has been dealing with catastrophic events worldwide. In 2002, the federal Department of Homeland Security (DHS) was developed to better coordinate emergency response, resources, and information. FEMA, along with 22 other agencies were moved under its control in hopes of better coordinating disaster response.

The terrorist attacks of September 11, 2001, the Space Shuttle Columbia disaster of 2003, and the devastating 2005 Hurricane Katrina, demonstrated the hazards that having a lack of common communication, management styles, or standardized resources can have on responses to emergencies. Soon thereafter, President Bush issued a directive that required the Department of Homeland Security to coordinate with other federal departments, state, local, and tribal governments to establish the National Incident Management System (NIMS). The adoption of the NIMS meant that finally, there would be one Incident Management System (IMS) for all agencies, specialties, and jurisdictions which would ensure efficient use of resources, clear communications, and better overall management.

> The ICS should be the backbone of all search operations regardless of their magnitude or duration

History of the Incident Command System

In the early 1970s, various public safety agencies in California responsible for responding to wildfires faced a compendium of difficulties including the following:

- Too many people reporting to one supervisor.
- Different emergency response organizational structures.
- Lack of reliable incident information.
- Inadequate and incompatible communications.
- Lack of a structure for coordinated planning between agencies.
- Unclear lines of authority.
- Terminology differences between agencies.
- Unclear or unspecified incident objectives.

For more information on HSPD 5 and HSPD 8 visit the following websites -
Homeland Security Presidential Directive 5
http://www.whitehouse.gov/news/releases/2003/02/20030228-9.html

Homeland Security Presidential Directive 8
http://www.whitehouse.gov/news/releases/2003/12/20031217-6.html

This directive establishes policies to strengthen the preparedness of the United States to prevent and respond to threatened or actual domestic terrorist attacks, major disasters, and other emergencies by requiring a national domestic all-hazards preparedness goal, establishing mechanisms for improved delivery of federal preparedness assistance to state and local governments, and outlining actions to strengthen preparedness capabilities of federal, state, and local entities.

The National Integration Center (NIC) Incident Management Systems Division was established by the Secretary of Homeland Security to provide "strategic direction for and oversight of the National Incident Management System (NIMS)... supporting both routine maintenance and the continuous refinement of the system and its components over the long term." The Center oversees all aspects of NIMS including the development of compliance criteria and implementation activities at federal, state and local levels. It provides guidance and support to jurisdictions and incident management and responder organizations as they adopt the system.

The Center is a multidisciplinary entity made up of federal stakeholders and, over time, it will include representatives of state, local and tribal incident management and responder organizations. It is situated within the Department of Homeland Security's Federal Emergency Management Agency.

The Incident Command System

In order to succeed the Incident Command System must meet the following characteristics:

- It must be organizationally flexible to expand and contract to meet the needs of the incident.
- It must be efficient to use on a day-to-day basis by all emergency response disciplines.
- It must use common terminology in order to allow personnel from various agencies and diverse geographic locations to meld rapidly into a common management structure.
- It must be cost effective.

Features of ICS (Fig. 2.1)

1. Common Terminology
2. Modular Organization
3. Chain of Command
4. Unity of Command
5. Unified Command
6. Span of Control
7. Pre-designated Incident Facilities
8. Resource Management
9. Integrated Communications
10. Transfer of Command

Incident Command Basics

Incident Command System (ICS) defines the operating characteristics, management components, and the structure of incident management and emergency response organizations engaged through the life cycle of an incident. As a component of NIMS, it is also the standardized management system used in search and rescue. From Maine to California, the language, organization, and function are the same. This discussion of ICS is certainly an introduction. With the integration of NIMS, many online courses have become readily available as well as classes across fire, rescue, and law enforcement disciplines.

Every incident has certain functions and objectives that must be performed, for example, a 4th of July celebration. It is an annual event for which Eric may be ultimately responsible; John will handle fireworks; Todd will handle parking; and Craig will handle setting up and breaking down bleachers, concessions, and toilet facilities. The type or size of the event does not matter, as certain activities and objectives will always apply.

The Five Functional Areas of the ICS
There are five functional areas in the Incident Command System which are:

1. Command
2. Operations
3. Planning
4. Logistics
5. Finance/Administration

The first arriving resource on the scene will establish the ICS and identify an Incident Command Post. Ideally, the most qualified person will assume command and all of the other functional responsibilities until they are delegated to someone else.

The roles and responsibilities of the functional areas:

Command
The Command function is primarily responsible for overall management of the incident. The Command is also responsible to ensure safety at the incident, create information channels to internal and external stakeholders, and establish liaison between agencies participating at the incident.

Command Staff
The Command Staff provide assistance in essential roles to the Incident Commander. They have the direct authority of the Incident Commander (IC). (See Fig. 2.2)

Fig. 2.2

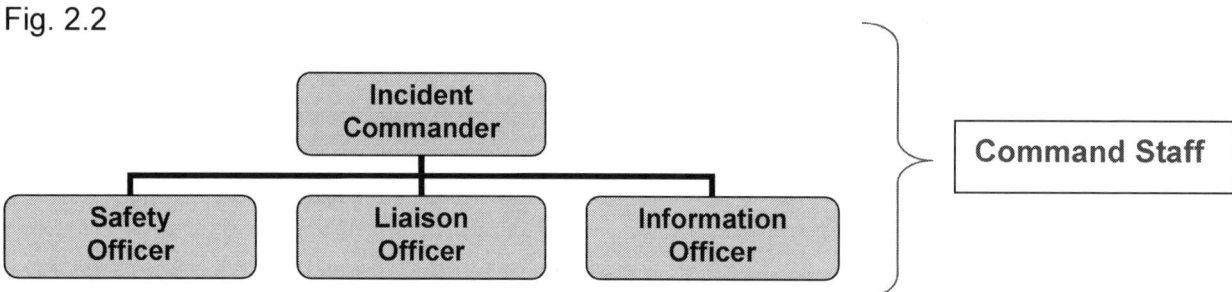

The Incident Command System can be structured as a "Single Command" or as a "Unified Command." Regardless of the ICS structure, the responsibilities remain the same. The IC must provide leadership for the incident. The IC may delegate authority to others; this is especially true in highly complex incidents and events. The IC generally follows guidelines and direction from their Agency Administrator. The IC has the ability to delegate the functions of Safety, Information, and Liaison to Officers and their functions are described below:

The **Safety Officer** works closely with the Incident Command and Operations Section Chief to ensure safety of all incident personnel. The Safety Officer can exercise authority to halt any unsafe operations. There will be only one Safety Officer for each operational period per incident.

The **Liaison Officer** assists the Incident Command by serving as the point of contact for agency representatives that are supporting the effort.

The **Information Officer** advises the Incident Command on disseminating information and media relations about the incident. The Information Officer will exchange information and intelligence with the Planning Section. The Incident Command must approve all information that the Information Officer releases.

General Staff
The General Staff consists of the four major activities of Operations, Planning, Logistics, and Finance/Administration.

The General Staff positions are referred to as Sections and the person in charge of each will be designated as a Section Chief. Section Chiefs may have a deputy. (See Fig. 2.3)

Fig. 2.3

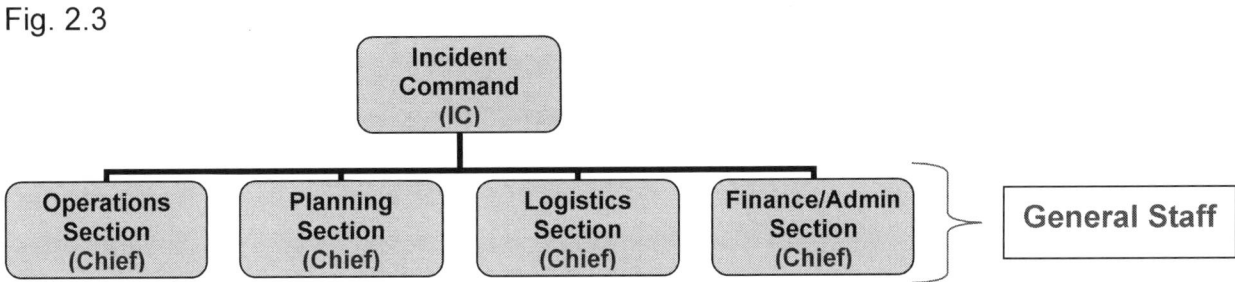

Operations Section
The Operations Section develops and implements the strategy and tactics used in order to achieve the incident objectives. Generally, the Operations Section is the first function that will be delegated by the Incident Commander. The Operation Section is also responsible for organizing, assigning, and supervising all tactical resources.

In order to maintain organization within the Operation Section, additional levels of organization can be used as necessary. They are:

- Single Resources
- Strike Teams
- Task Forces
- Groups
- Divisions
- Branches

Resource Management
During an incident, resources must be managed and accounted for at all times. The ICS manages resources by organizing them in the following ways:

Single Resource - A single resource is the smallest unit that can operate independently with common communications and supervisor. An example of a single resource is a K9 and handler. A motorcycle <u>without a driver</u> is not a single resource because it can't operate itself.

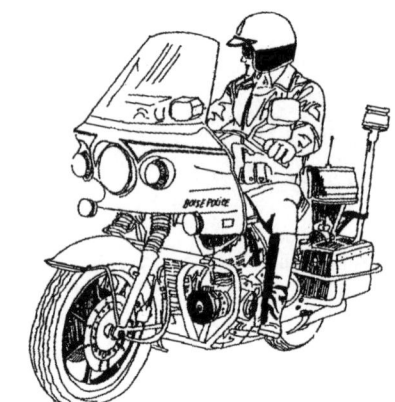

Strike Team - A strike team is a combination of the same kind and type of resource with common communications and a leader. A strike team will consist of several common single resources.

Task Force - A task force is any combination of different resources, assembled for a specific task, with common communications and a leader. Example is helicopter, K9 with handler, ground search team, and a technical rescue team assigned to work together in a designated area under the direction of a leader.

Groups divide incident resources into <u>functional</u> areas.

Divisions organize incident resources by <u>geographical</u> areas.

Branches have functional or geographical responsibility for major parts of the incident operations.

RESTAT (Resource Status) is another way to manage and account for resources by assigning status conditions. Resources at an incident will always be in one of these conditions:

- Available – Resource awaiting an active assignment.
- Assigned – Resource has been assigned and is preparing for or actively engaged in their assignment.
- Out of Service – Resource is on site but not assigned and not available.

Planning Section

The Planning Section is responsible for establishing the Incident Action Plan (IAP), collecting and evaluating the incident situation. The Planning Section is the "think-tank" in the management team and determines alternate strategies. The Planning Section has a number of vital functions including:

- Maintaining resource status (RESTAT).
- Maintaining and displaying situation status. Incident Situational Status (SITSTAT).
- Preparing the written Incident Action Plan.
- Providing documentation services.
- Preparing the Demobilization Plan (large complexity incidents).
- Providing search investigation and intelligence.
- Providing a primary location for technical specialists assigned to the incident. (Fig. 2.4)

While it is important to delegate authority for an Operations Section, at large scaled incidents such as a search, it is extremely valuable to establish a Planning Section early on in the incident.

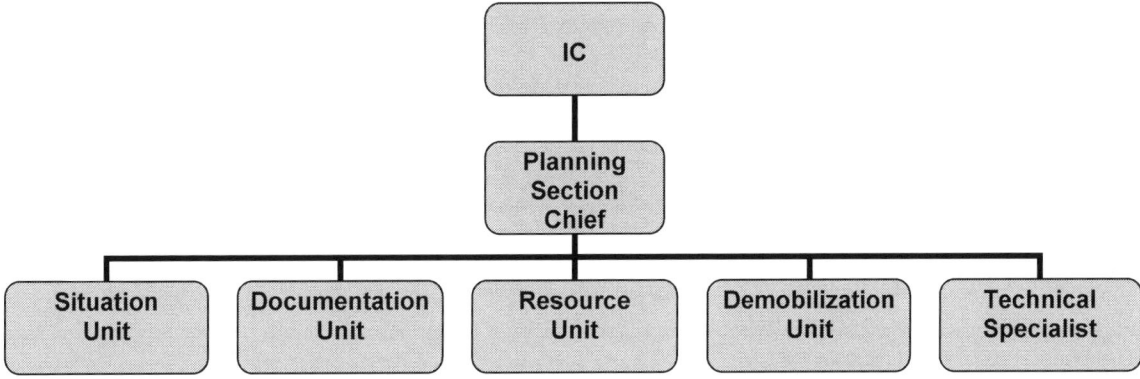

Fig. 2.4

Logistic Section

The Logistic Section is responsible for all services and support needs of an incident including facilities, equipment, supplies, and personnel. The Logistic Section can be expanded to two branches with each having three units if needed; they are – (Fig. 2.5)

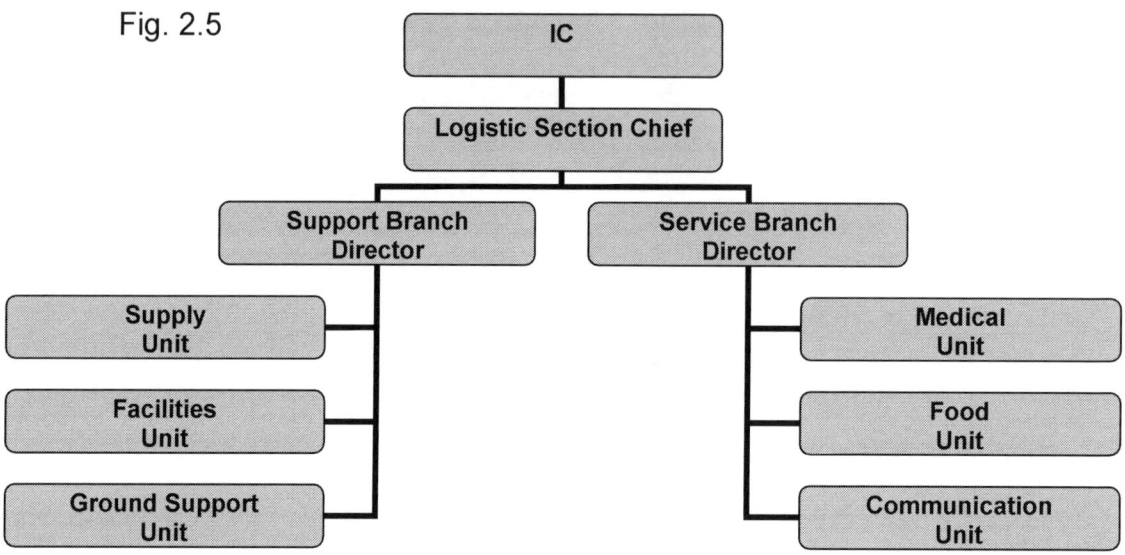

Fig. 2.5

Finance/Administration Section

The Finance/Administration Section is responsible for all financial activities related to the incident such as procurement, claims, time recording and cost analysis. The Finance/Administration Section is used for any incident that may require on-site financial management. While this function can be performed by the IC at small complex incidents, it is beneficial to delegate this activity to others during large complex incidents.

The Finance/Administration Section can be expanded to four units if necessary; they are – (Fig. 2.6)

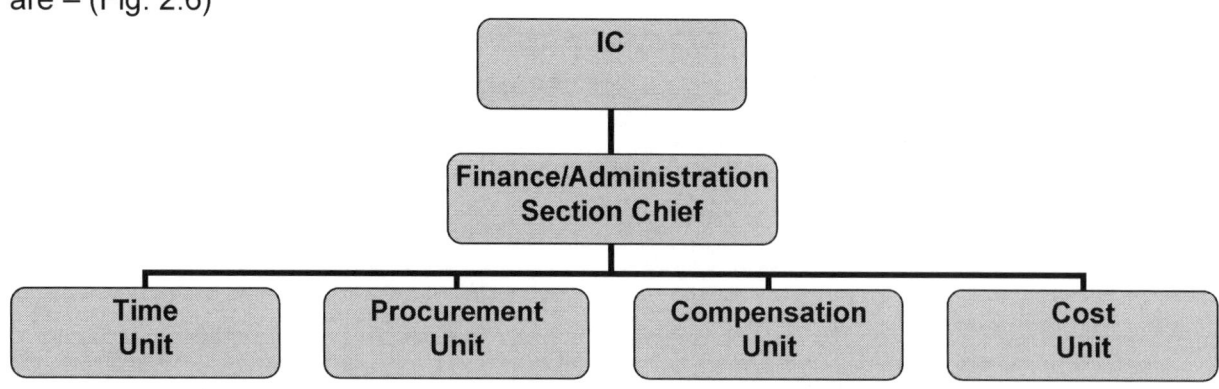

Fig. 2.6

Features of ICS

The following features are specific to the ICS and make it the desirable system used by SAR and emergency professionals all over the United States and beyond. These characteristics illustrate the benefit of having standardized guidelines. (See Fig. 2.1)

Common Terminology

Imagine walking into a foreign country and attempting to communicate with someone. Having clear, concise terminology established will help an incident run smoothly regardless of the location or type of incident. The key to this characteristic in the United States is to use plain English; in other words, no codes or jargon. Ten codes, for example, are not standard across counties, let alone states. In ICS, using common terminology helps define:

A. Organizational Elements
B. Incident Facilities
C. Resources
D. Position Titles

Incident Facilities: Facilities are established depending on the size and complexity of the incident. Their names and function are standard regardless of the type of incident. The following are common facilities:

Incident Command Post – The location from which the Incident Command oversees all incident operations and where primary command functions are performed. There is only one ICP for each event and is collocated with the Incident Base.

Staging Areas – Temporary locations where resources are kept while awaiting incident assignment. Most large incidents will have a staging area and some may have several. These are managed by a Staging Area Manager who reports to the Operations Section Chief or Incident Commander if an Operations Section has not been established.

Incident Base – The location where primary service and support activities are performed. The base is different than staging areas in that resources stationed there are generally out-of-service as compared to those in the staging are that are "available."

Helibase – Staffed area where helicopters may land, re-fuel, and be maintained.

Helispots – Temporary locations where helicopters can land, load and off-load personnel, equipment, and supplies.

Resources: Personnel and major items of equipment for which status is maintained. Common designations are assigned to various resources and may be classified by kind (what the resource is: i.e. medic, firefighter, ambulance, helicopter) and type (size, capability, and staffing qualifications of a specific kind of resource).

Position Titles: Management positions within the ICS structure are referred to by title such as Chief, Officer, Director, or Supervisor. By using specific titles, it ensures using the most qualified personnel without the confusion of multi-agency rank designations. (See Fig. 2.7)

ICS Organizational Elements (Fig. 2.7)

Primary Position	Title
Incident Commander	Incident Commander
Command Staff	Officer
Section	Chief
Branch	Director
Division/Group	Supervisor
Strike Team/Task Force	Leader
Unit	Leader
Single Resource	Unit Designation

Modular Organization

The ICS structure expands in a top-down modular fashion. When there is too much to handle, functions are divided and assigned to different individuals. In other words, the organization is based on the size and complexity of the incident (See Fig.2.7).

These positions are only broken out when there is a need and each element must have a person in charge.

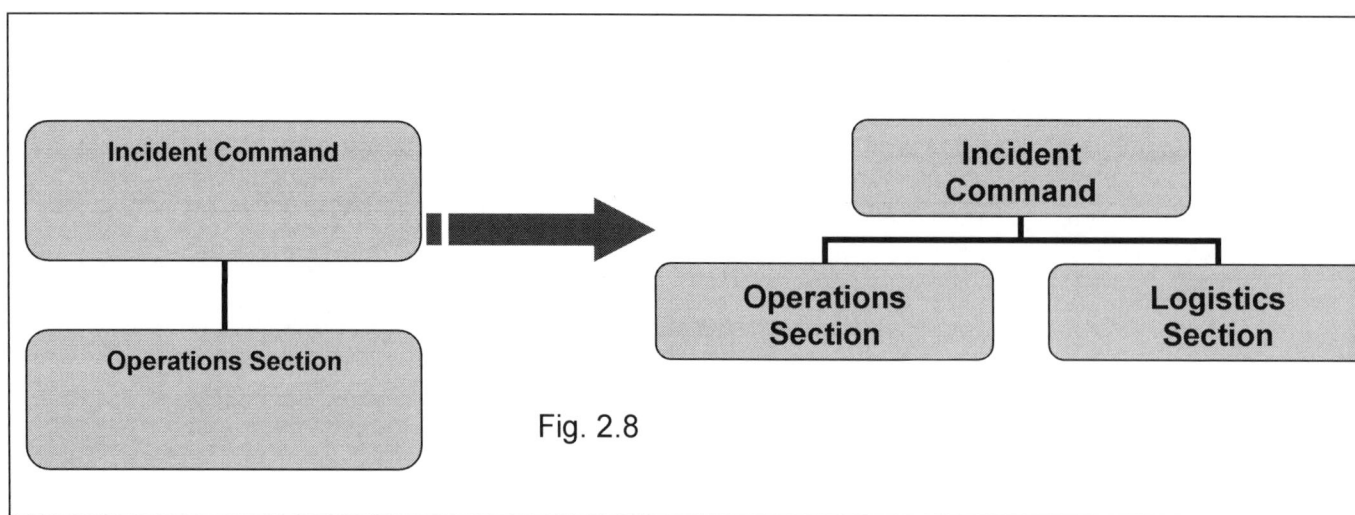

Fig. 2.8

Chain of Command
The Chain of Command refers to a clear and orderly line of authority within the ranks of the incident management organization. (See Fig. 2.9)

Fig. 2.9

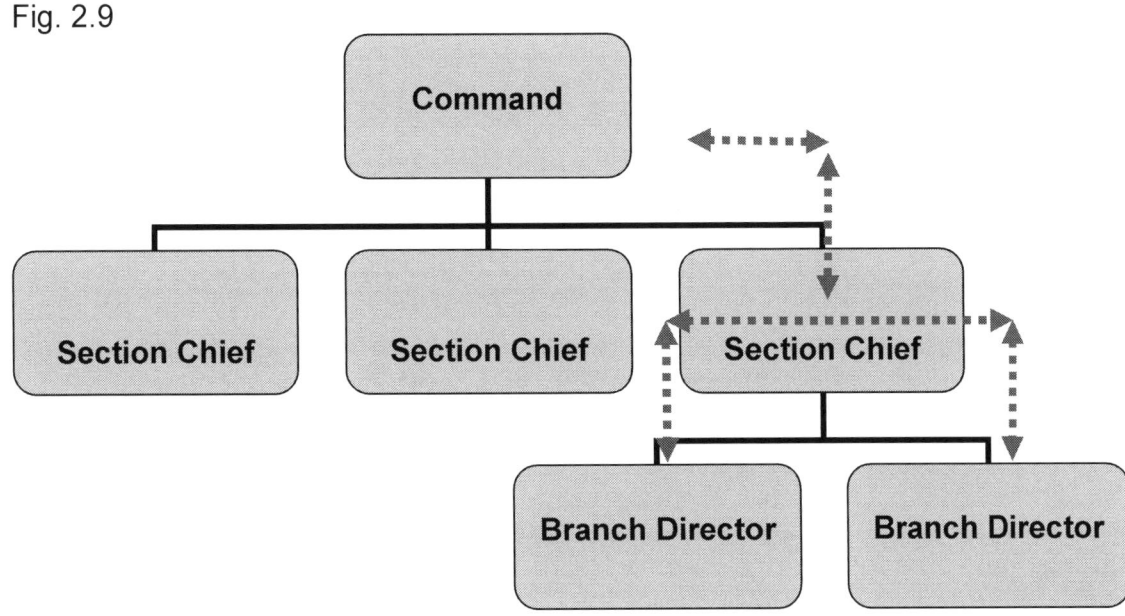

> **Unity of Command**
>
> The Unity of Command means that every person in the organization has a single designated supervisor with whom they report. Do not confuse "Unity of Command" with "Unified Command" [Unity of Command means that each person will be given one supervisor and they should not expect to be given information, assignments, or direction from any other than their immediate supervisor.]

Span of Control
Search and Rescue personnel are constantly demonstrating leadership and followership characteristics. In order to use resources proficiently, attention needs to be focused on the number of individuals that one leader can manage. ICS considers an "effective span of control" to be a ratio of one supervisor/leader to three to seven subordinates; however, the ratio of one to five is optimum. If it falls outside of those ranges, expansion or consolidation of the organization, using resource management techniques, may be used to branch out, group together or divide.

How does ICS fit into Search and Rescue?

When the first responding resources arrive on the scene, establishing the Incident Command contributes to a successful outcome of finding the subject by identifying objectives and various strategies. Establishing a command structure also contributes to maintaining safety and accountability on everyone supporting the incident. Searching for missing persons inherently exposes the personnel to a higher risk simply due to the fact that these personnel are going to be leaving the direct supervision of command and possibly covering large geographical areas. The need for accountability forces leadership to know who is where and why, when they are supposed to return, what communication frequency they will be on, etc.

Upon arrival on the scene, some of the initial responsibilities of responders will be to account for personnel through sign-in logs, determine the urgency of the situation, identify where the missing person was last seen or known to have been, and gather a physical description of the missing person. Additionally, someone needs to assure that no unnecessary personnel enter and contaminate the likely areas where the subject was known to have been.

While the list of management tasks expands, the Incident Commander still needs to identify these jobs that need to be completed. It is important to establish who the responsible authority is, identify the incident commander, and establish the operations and planning sections early. Operations should quickly identify a staging area for incoming resources.

ICS and NIMS Training

Many agencies have been required to meet federal requirements by ensuring that first responders to any type of incident complete a series of NIMS training. At the time of the release of this book, there were six courses that are required in order for an individual or organization to be considered NIMS compliant.

FEMA IS 700 – Introduction to NIMS
FEMA IS 800 – Introduction to National Response Framework (NFR)
ICS-100 [I-100] – Introduction to ICS
ICS-200 [I-200] – Basic ICS
ICS-300 [I-300] – Intermediate to ICS
ICS-400 [I-400] – Advanced ICS

While most of these training programs are available online, ICS-300 and ICS-400 are classroom-required classes.

Personnel Training Requirements
   Entry Level
      IS-700 and ICS-100

   First Line, Single Resource, Field Supervisors
      IS-700, ICS-100 and ICS-200

   Mid-level Management: Strike Team Leaders, Division Supervisors, etc.
      IS-700, IS-800.B NRF, ICS-100, ICS-200 and ICS-300

   Command and General Staff, Area, Emergency and EOC Managers
      IS-700, IS-800.B, ICS-100, ICS-200, ICS-300 and ICS-400

ICS Forms

Another characteristic of the standardization of the ICS features is that the forms are also standardized.

See the appendix for some of the most commonly used forms and the forms that are used to make up the incident action plan (IAP).

ICS Form Name
ICS 201 - Incident Briefing form:
Page 1 - Incident Briefing / Map Sketch
Page 2 - Summary of Current Actions
Page 3 - Current Organization
Page 4 - Resources Summary
ICS 202 - Incident Objectives List
ICS 203 - Organization Assignment List
ICS 204 - Division Assignment List
ICS 205 - Incident Radio Communications Plan
ICS 206 - Medical Plan
ICS 207 - Organizational Chart (requires legal size paper)
ICS 209 - Incident Status Summary Report
ICS 210 - Status Change Card
ICS 211 - Incident Check-In Lists
ICS 213 - General Message form
ICS 214 - Unit Log Form
ICS 215 - Operational Planning Worksheet
ICS 215A - Incident Safety Worksheet
ICS 216 - Radio Requirements Worksheet
ICS 217 - Radio Frequency Assignment Worksheet
ICS 218 - Support Vehicle Inventory form
ICS 219 - Resource Status Card
ICS 219-2 - Crew (green)
ICS 219-4 - Helicopter (blue)
ICS 219-6 - Aircraft (orange)
ICS 219-7 - Dozer (yellow)
ICS 220 - Air Operations Summary
ICS 221 - Demobilization Checkout and Instructions

Alaska Mountain Rescue Group **INCIDENT BRIEFING** ICS-201	Date: *SAT 17 MAY 2008*	IC: *Sgt. Joe Thursday APD*
	Mission: *Missing person* *Katie Brown, 15*	Case No.: *08-8888888*

MAP/AREA SKETCH:

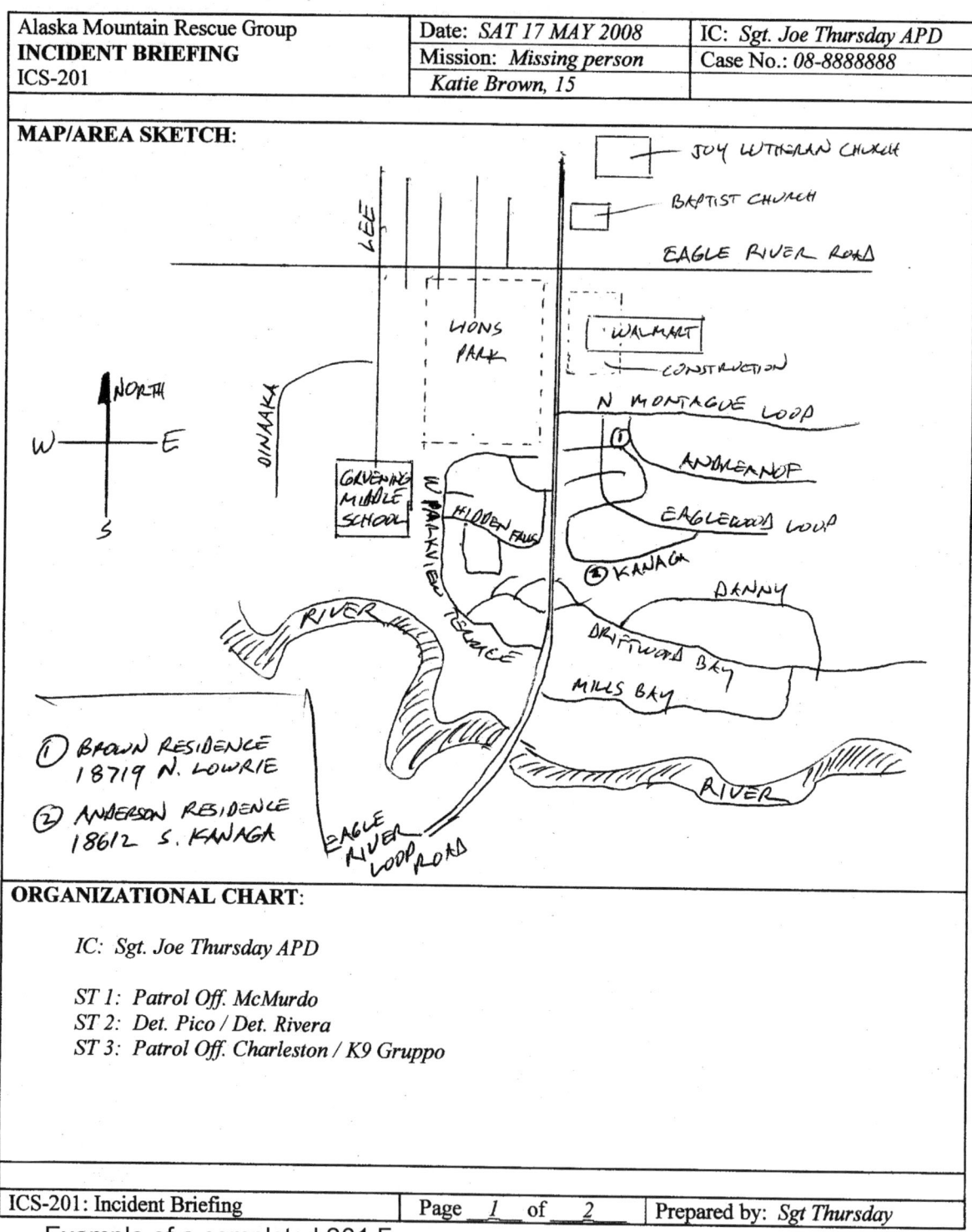

ORGANIZATIONAL CHART:

IC: *Sgt. Joe Thursday APD*

ST 1: *Patrol Off. McMurdo*
ST 2: *Det. Pico / Det. Rivera*
ST 3: *Patrol Off. Charleston / K9 Gruppo*

ICS-201: Incident Briefing	Page _1_ of _2_	Prepared by: *Sgt Thursday*

Example of a completed 201 Form

CURRENT RESOURCE LOG:						
No.	Name	Type	Quantity	MOB Day	MOB Time	Location
01	McMurdo	Patrol	1	5/17	0705	Brown residence
02	Thursday	Sgt	1	5/17	0712	Anderson residence
03	Pico / Rivera	Det	2	5/17	0740	Anderson residence
04	Charleston / Gruppo	K9 unit	1	5/17	0820	Lions Park
05						
06						

SUMMARY OF CURRENT ACTIONS:

0705 — 911 call from parents -- Katie Brown, 15, missing.
Subject last seen approx 2045 Friday 5/16 at home, w/ overnight bag
Brown's parents say subject supposed to overnight w/ Maddie Anderson, 15. Not there at 0700 today.
Brown residence: 18719 North Lowrie Loop

Anderson's parents say that was last weekend / no plans for this weekend.
Anderson residence: 18612 South Kanaga Loop

0712 — ST 1 arrives Brown res – interview, search, remain w/ parents
5'0", 97 pounds, brown hair, blue eyes, pierced ears, no tattoos
9th grade at ER high, attended Gruening Middle School
No answer on subject's cell phone – goes to voice mail.
0717 — Sgt Thursday arrives Anderson res / assumes command / quick search of neighborhood
0740 — ST 2 arrives Anderson res, begins interviews / search / photos
0747 — Sgt Thursday requests APD search team, all available searchers, dogs, incident management team
0820 — ST 3 arrives, assigned to hasty search Lions Park & Gruening school outdoor areas
0833 — ST 2 to WalMart, hasty search of store, review of security tapes 2030 Friday to present
0845 — Joy Lutheran Church offers parking lot & building for staging / command
0850 — Sgt Thursday preparing ICS form 201 for handoff to incident management team

ICS-201: Incident Briefing — Page 2 of 2 — Prepared by: Sgt. Thursday

Example of a completed 201 Form

Chapter 2 Review Questions

1. List the five functional areas of the ICS.

    a) _____
    b) _____
    c) _____
    d) _____
    e) _____

2. List the four General Staff positions.

    a) _____
    b) _____
    c) _____
    d) _____

3. List the three resource status conditions.

    a) _____
    b) _____
    c) _____

4. For each of the organizational elements listed below on the left, designate the number of the appropriate ICS title.

    _____ Branch   1. Leader
    _____ Section   2. Officer
    _____ Division   3. Supervisor
    _____ Command Staff   4. Chief
    _____ Strike Team   5. Director

5. The optimum span of control is what ratio?

   1 to ____ (leaders to subordinates)

6. The Command staff consists of the following four elements.

   a) _____
   b) _____
   c) _____
   d) _____

7. What is the definition of a "Strike Team"?

   _____
   _____
   _____
   _____

8. What is the definition of a "Single Resource"?

   _____
   _____
   _____
   _____

9. What is the responsibility of the Liaison Officer?

   _____
   _____
   _____

Using the Aguinaldo Search Scenario
- Identify on the map where the ICP should be located. [ICS 201]
- Have the group use the ICS Form 211 for the Check-In.
- Identify what ICS organization would be establish. [ICS 201]
- Identify Incident Objectives. [ICS 201]
- Complete the necessary ICS forms to support the module organization.

Group Activity (30 mins)

Aguinaldo Scenario
Mr. Magtanggol Aguinaldo is an 87-year-old male who was visiting with relatives for a funeral. Mr. Aguinaldo's wife called 911 after they could not locate him this morning. The first arriving patrol car arrived at 12:30 hours.

Mrs. Aguinaldo informs the Police Officer that they are from Bacolod, Philippines and that her husband has diabetes and dementia. She last saw him sitting on the front porch of her nephew's home. She said that she went inside to take a nap and when she returned he was no longer there.

Chapter 3 –

Introduction to Basic Land Navigation

Chapter 3 Introduction to Basic Land Navigation
- Importance of Orienting
- Different Types of Maps
- Compass
- Measuring Distance by Pace
- Georeferencing
- Map Exercise(s)

Upon completion of this chapter and the related course activities, the student will be able to meet the following objectives:

- Describe the various methods used to navigate.
- Describe the different types of compasses.
- Describe the basic features of an orienteering compass.
- Demonstrate the "waist-high" and "eye-level" techniques used to determine a bearing.
- Describe the differences between the various types of maps used in search and rescue.
- Demonstrate measuring distance by pace count.
- Demonstrate the understanding of the two types of geo referencing systems
    - Latitude and Longitude
    - United States National Grid

Chapter 3 – Introduction to Basic Land Navigation

Importance of Being Geographically Oriented

Most people have a basic good general sense of direction when it comes down to their geographical location. At some point in time we all find ourselves asking questions like: Where am I? Where am I going? How long will it take for me to get there? How do I get back? When we are driving somewhere these questions may be raised but we have the advantage of identifiable landmarks and street signs to assist us. When we enter the wilderness environment we certainly lose most, if not all, of the navigation aids that we take for granted in our routine life. During and after a disaster, common landmarks and street signs that normally assist us can be destroyed or non-existent.

Most trails have markings for recreational hikers to follow. But the problem arises for search and rescue personnel because they will have to operate in areas without markings. In survival training there are a number of tricks of the trade. An example is the old adage that moss only grows on the north side of the tree. It does have merit depending upon where the tree is in relation to majority of sunlight. For example in the middle latitudes of the northern hemisphere, the south sides of things get more sunlight during the year and moss generally does not like sunlight. This information is certainly useful and in a survival situation may make the difference between life and death, but I would much rather depend on a compass. So the search and rescuer must master navigation and map orientation skills. The tools of the trade for navigation primarily consist of a compass and map.

> *I can't rightly say I've ever been lost, but I've been mighty perplexed for two or three days runnin'*
>
> – Davy Crockett
> 1786 – 1836

We can use a number of different methods to navigate or simply know where we are such as:

- Celestial navigation – observing the sun, moon, stars, and planets.
- Pilotage – using visible natural and manmade features such as sea marks and beacons.
- Dead reckoning – using course and speed to determine position.
- Off-course navigation – allows for variables in heading by deliberately aiming to the one side of the destination. (Also referred to as "aiming off" or "off-set aiming")
- Electronic navigation – using electronic equipment such as radio navigation and satellite navigation system (GPS) to follow a course to a location.

The first method used to navigate was Celestial but the problem arose when fog and clouds appeared, obscuring visibility of the planets, sun, and stars.

Today's modern compass is a great deal more precise and offers to a large extent more added features such as phosphorescent parts that can be seen in the dark, rotating bezel, orienting lines, mirror, etc.

There are numerous types of compasses developed for specific needs, uses, and accuracies:

- Floating-Dial Type
- Cruiser Type
- Fixed-Dial Type
- Orienteering Type

Floating-Dial Type   Cruiser Type   Fixed-Dial Type   Orienteering Type

Fixed-Dial **compasses** are typically the kind found in gumball machines and cereal boxes. They are generally not accurate enough for search activities but certainly are acceptable in survival situations, and searchers should be familiar with them.

Orienteering **compasses** are the ideal choice in search and rescue because of the additional features that allow for easier use than other types of compasses.

Floating-Dial **compasses** have the dial freely spinning on the pivot. There are no rotating bezels that need to be adjusted. These also include lensatic compasses.

Cruiser **type compasses** are high-priced compasses that generally provide exceptionally accuracy. They are normally used by foresters, geologists and maritime; they can be waterproof.

An orienteering compass includes the following basic parts:

- Scales
- Base Plate
- Direction of Travel Arrow
- Magnifier
- Index Pointer
- Rotating Dial
- Declination Marks
- Orienting Arrow
- Orienting Lines
- Magnetic Needle
- Sighting Mirror (below)

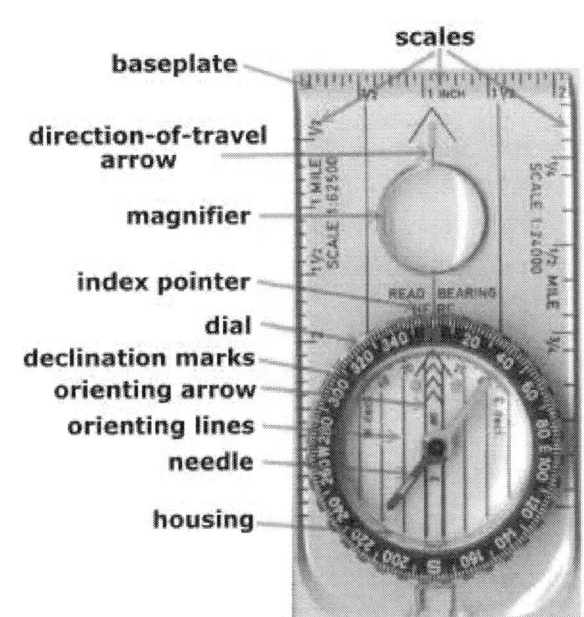

The base plate is usually clear, but can be yellow or black. It is rectangular with edge measurement markings and scales.

The rotating bezel (as shown) is marked clockwise in 360 degrees; it is preferable that compasses used by searchers should be marked in 1° or 2-degree increments. The orienting lines on the bottom of the capsule inside the rotating bezel are used with a map to obtain navigational headings. Most compasses also have an outline of a compass arrow (also within the dial) or possibly two marks near the north end of the capsule. These items are used to align the magnetic needle with the orienting arrow so that a bearing can be followed in the outdoor setting. This has informally been called the "box" or "dog house."

The magnetic needles for most compasses have the red or night-visible ends of the needle pointing towards magnetic north. In high quality compasses, the magnetic needle usually pivots on a jeweled bearing for smooth action. To help the needle move smoothly and settle quickly, the dial is filled with a non-freezing liquid to reduce shakiness.

The direction of travel arrow is a line inscribed in the base plate of the compass, the base of which forms the index line (or, if you are on a ship, referred to as a "lubber line"). It is important to know that the direction of travel arrow should always be pointing in the desired direction of travel while navigating.

The index line is located where the degree reading (also referred to as an azimuth) is read, usually at the bottom of the direction-of-travel arrow. The index line can also be referred to as the "index mark."

The sighting mirror is usually on a hinged cover of the compass, which has a fine line that runs from top to bottom at the center of the mirror. This center line is an extension of the direction-of-travel arrow and allows the compass to be used more accurately at eye level.

Before we start talking about using the compass, let's discuss headings. Most of us focus on North, South, East, and West, which we refer to as the cardinal points or directions. A compass rose (see Fig. 3.1) is graduated in 360 degrees and the cardinal points are separated by 90 degrees starting at 0 degrees being north, 90 degrees is east, 180 degrees is south, 270 degrees is west, and we find ourselves back at 360 or 0 degrees again at North. North can also be referred to as 360 degrees.

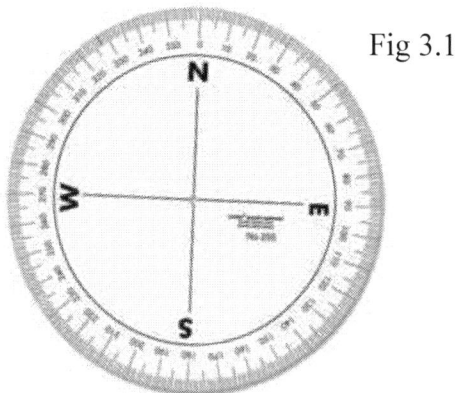

Fig 3.1

We can add cardinal points by using North East (NE) being 45°, South East (SE) 135°, South West (SW) 225°, and North West (NW) 315°. However, it is preferable to provide only the numerical value of degree heading in order to achieve your desired direction.

For example, if you are asked to take a 270-degree heading, which cardinal point would you be heading?

Try the following exercises:

1. For a 360-degree heading, which cardinal point would you be heading?
   _____

2. For a 90-degree heading, which cardinal point would you be heading?
   _____

3. For a 180-degree heading, which cardinal point would you be heading?
   _____

4. For a 315-degree heading, which cardinal point would you be heading?
   _____

5. For a 225-degree heading, which cardinal point would you be heading?
   _____

6. For a 45-degree heading, which cardinal point would you be heading?
   _____

7. For a 135-degree heading, which cardinal point would you be heading?
   _____

8. If we asked you to take a 270 degree heading, which cardinal point would you be heading? _____

Determining a Bearing for an Object in the Field

There are two methods to determine a navigational bearing: the "waist-high" and the "eye level". The method used is based on the type of compass being used, either with or without a sighting mirror.

Fig 3.2

Waist-High Method:
   Determining a bearing of an object:
   1. Hold the compass in front of you between waist-high and chest-high. Be sure to keep the compass level and not tilted, this will keep the needle from contacting the top of the capsule and affecting the heading. It is also important to stand straight and in-line with your direction of travel,

elbows close to your body. This position assures that as you turn your body and compass toward the object that you will be in-line with the object and on a correct compass heading.

2. Holding the compass level, with one hand, rotate the bezel until the "N" on the bezel is aligned with the red end of the magnetic needle. Note that the "orienteering lines" are indeed parallel with the magnetic needle.

Step 1

Step 2

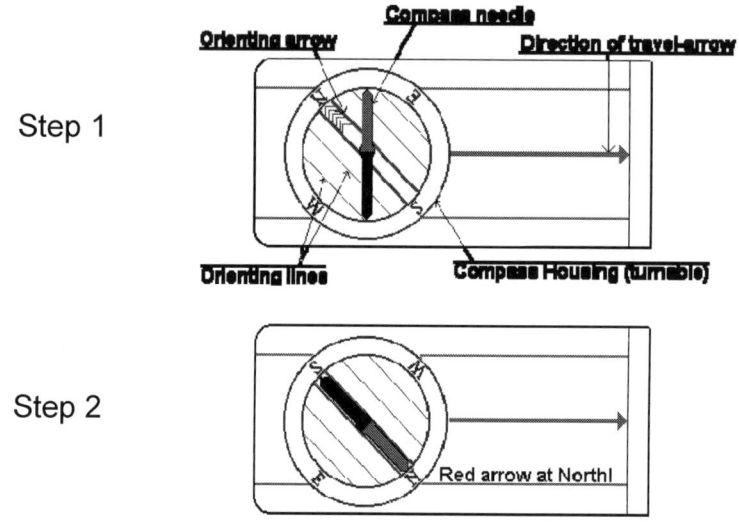

www.learn-orienteering.org/old/img/compass1.gif

3. Move the compass from the chest-high position in order to read the bearing to the object. The bearing to the object is the number of degrees on the bezel that is aligned with the index line, which is an extension of the direction of travel arrow.

4. Note: any ferrous metal near the compass needle will distort the reading.

Eye Level Method:
Bring the compass up to your eye. Position it so that you can see the object in the notch at the top of the mirror. While keeping the bezel level, rotate the bezel until the North-pointing needle is boxed or inside the outline on the capsule. Align the vertical index line and object all in the same line. Fine-tune the bezel to keep the needle boxed. Read the degree at the intersection of the bezel and index line.

Following a Compass Heading:
Set the desired degree on the bezel at the index line, holding the compass level. Rotate your body and the compass as one until you box the needle. Find an object in the field that lines up with the index line and use it as a landmark.

Maps – Tools for Navigation

A map is a pictorial representation of the Earth's surface drawn to scale and reproduced on a flat piece of paper.

There are a variety of maps and charts, but for search and rescue, a map should adequately reflect the terrain within the search area. It also needs to have the appropriate amount of detail of the area for those traveling on foot. For a wilderness search, the use of a topographical map is most appropriate; for an urban search a planimetric map may be the most appropriate; for an air search for a missing plane, an aeronautical chart/map would be the most appropriate; and for a water search of a bay, river, or lake, a nautical chart/map would be the most appropriate. Generally, a topographic map is the map of choice for search and rescue.

As a minimum, maps for land navigation should provide the following data:

- An accurate depiction of terrain in a scale that is realistic for resources.
- The major terrain features such as hills, valleys, and ridges.
- "Man-made" features such as buildings, trails, and roads.
- An accurate depiction of measurable relief, elevation, and contour (lay of the land).
- A georeferencing coordinate system (Latitude/Longitude, UTM, and/or USNG)
- The location of water and water courses.

Maps are an essential part of any search activity. There are various types of maps, all of which may be valuable at the search incident. Some examples of map types include:

- Planimetric Maps
- Topographic Maps
- Nautical Charts
- Aeronautical Charts
- Orthophoto Maps
- Relief Maps
- Hydrologic Maps
- Geologic Maps
- Hybrid (satellite or aerial)

***Planimetric* maps** (Fig. 3.3) are two dimensional maps and are the most common type of map used by most people in urban settings. These are basically street maps. They illustrate horizon positions on the map but not any vertical information. Planimetric maps illustrate roads, buildings, parks, lakes and rivers and are usually labeled. Most people are accustomed to these types of maps simply because of their availability and usefulness in everyday activities. The better-drawn maps are scaled, where a given distance anywhere on the map represents the distance in the field. They also indicate

North and have a key to identify the symbols used on the map. These maps are usually drawn to a scale that provides a reasonable trade-off of coverage with detail for navigating by automobile.

Fig. 3.3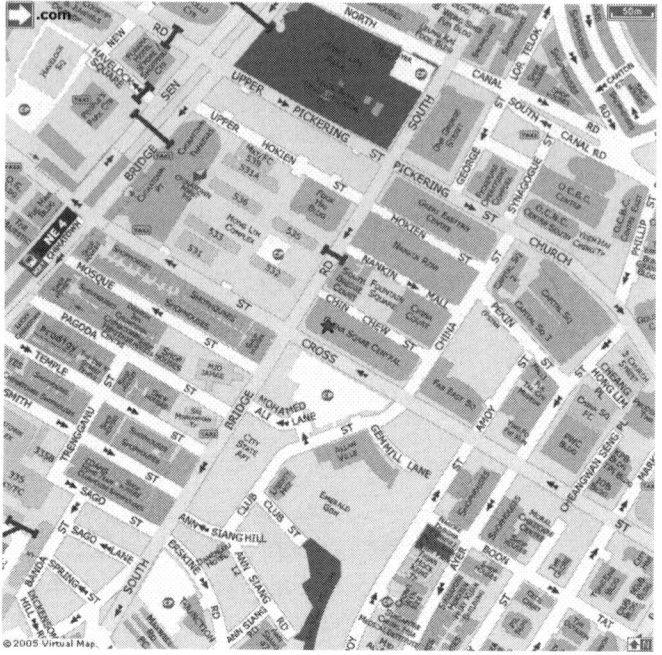

***Topographic* maps** (Fig. 3.4) portray the shape and elevation of the terrain while showing a graphic representation of selected man-made and natural features plotted to scale. These maps are generally used in search incidents because of the detailed information it affords both the search management and field resources.

The U.S. Geological Survey or USGS produces 7.5 minute, 1:24,000 scale topographic maps. The map covers an area of 7.5 minutes of latitude and longitude distance at a 1:24,000 scale. A scale of 1:24,000 indicates that one inch on the map represents 24,000 inches or 2,000 feet on the ground or within the area depicted on the map.

Additionally, brown lines (referred to as contour lines) represent terrain elevation and generally have intervals of 20, 40, 80, or 200 feet as stated in the legend at the bottom of the map. There are several types of contour lines; two of them are index and intermediate. An index countour line will indicate the elevation numerically on the line in feet above mean sea level (MSL) and is every fifth line with four intermediate lines in between every two index lines.

Because so much information is contained on a standard USGS topographic map, a common symbol set is used. Unfortunately, because the symbol set is so expansive, only a few of the symbols are shown in the legend's lower right collar or border area. A complete set of symbol legends can be viewed and/or purchased from the USGS at http://erg.usgs.gov/isb/pubs/booklets/symbols/

Even without the secondary legend, one can infer quite a lot just by the color of the symbol. Generally, man-made permanent objects like buildings, railroad tracks, telephone lines, and roads are shown in **Black** – though some major roads and built up areas (towns and cities) are shown in **Red**. Water features such as lakes, rivers, and streams are shown in **Blue**. Contour lines and some other "earth features" are drawn in **Brown**. **Green** is used to depict areas of denser vegetation in contrast to less dense areas that are shown in **White**. **White** also may indicate cultivated or cleared areas. Items drawn in **Purple** are updates.

Fig. 3.4

***Nautical* charts** show maritime and coastal regions. They provide pilots of ships with information necessary to navigate on the waterways and safely avoid hazards that may be hidden under the water's surface. They usually depict depth, seabed features, some wrecks, tides, currents and navigational aids. (Fig. 3.5)

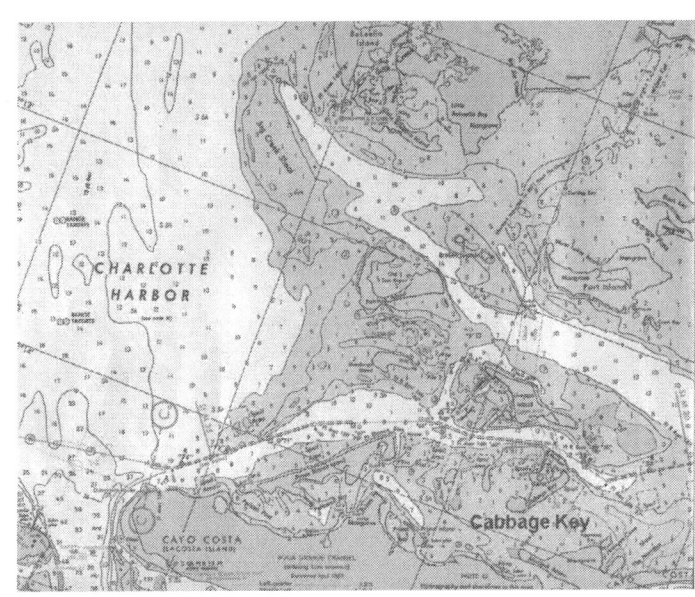

Fig 3.5

***Aeronautical* charts** aid aircraft pilots by showing small-scale topography, heights of potential obstructions the aircraft may encounter, flight patterns and lanes, and airports. (Fig. 3.6)

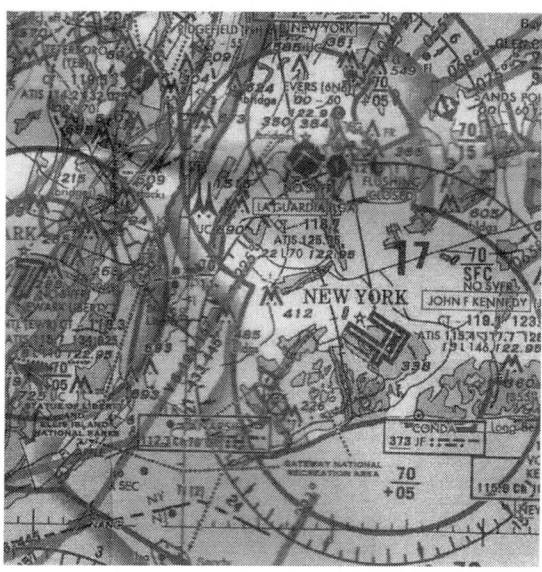

Fig. 3.6

***Orthophoto* maps** illustrate features of the land by using color-enhanced photographic images that have been processed to show detail in true position. They may include elevation changes and some man-made feature labeling. (Fig. 3.7)

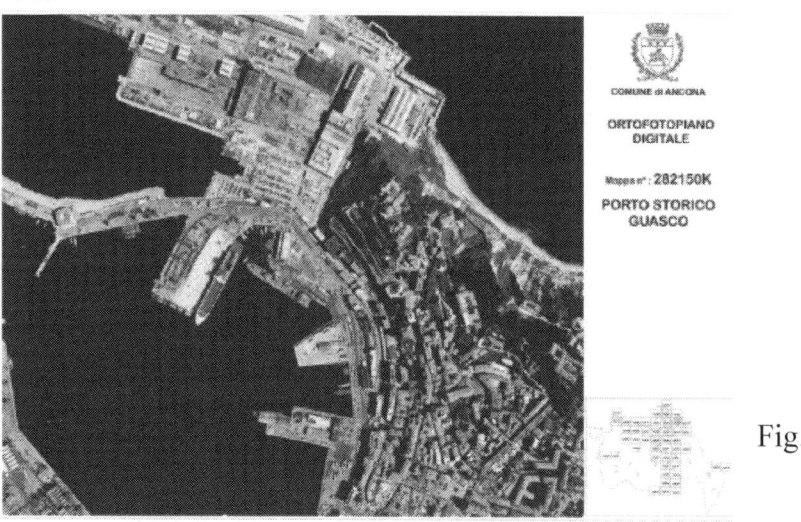

Fig. 3.7

***Relief* maps** show colors, shading, and contour lines outlining the terrain elevation and general features. (Fig. 3.8)

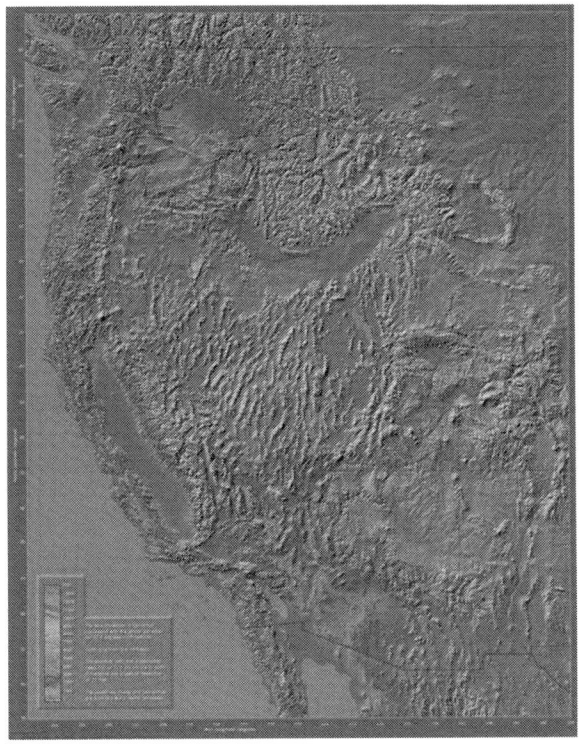

Fig. 3.8

***Hydrologic* maps** generally show the network of natural waterways within the targeted area of the map. (Fig. 3.9)

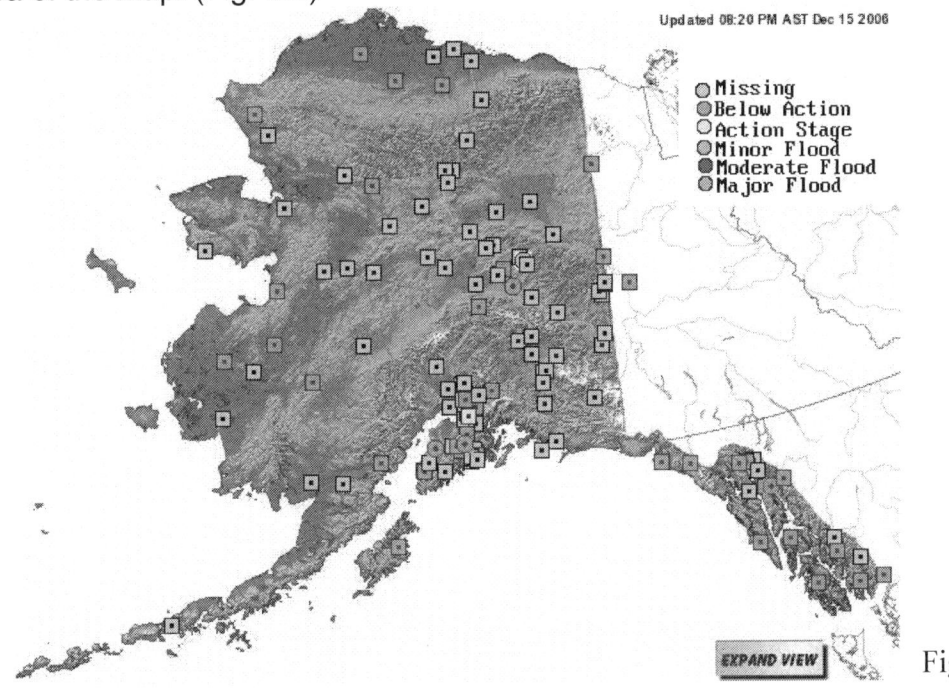

Fig. 3.9

***Geologic* maps** illustrate what is on and below the earth's surface such as the distribution of various rocks, soil, the earth's mantle, fault lines, and landslides. (Fig. 3.10)

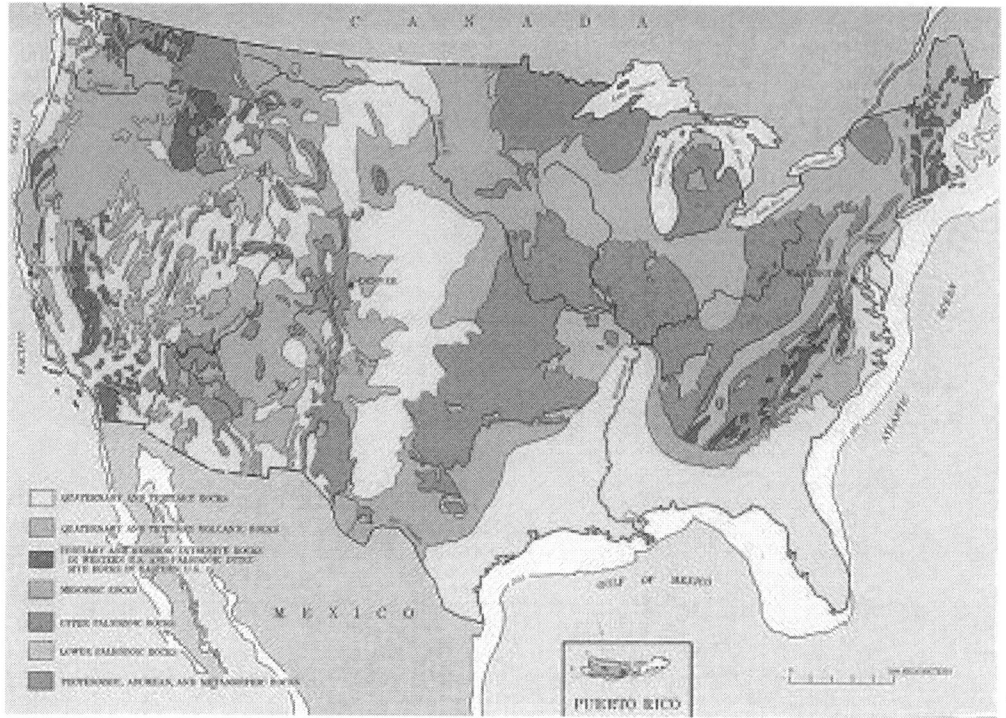

Fig. 3.10

Measuring Distance by Pace

Keeping track of your distance traveled is essential in search and rescue. In order to find where you are using a map, you can find prominent landmarks and features that can be distinguished both in the field and on your map. Or, you can locate your starting point on the map and follow a known heading and approximate distance and use that data to calculate your location on the map. Location plotting is also beneficial at a search incident to identify and document where a clue is located. The second method is preferred since it does not rely on terrain features.

Distance can be estimated by knowing the length of one's pace, stride (a person's double step) and multiplying it by the number of paces/strides taken.

The English term "mile" is derived from a Roman term which means "1,000 Roman Paces" or double steps. The Romans considered the pace to be five times the length of a Roman legionnaire's foot and, thus, the Roman mile was 5,000 feet. It wasn't until much later that the English mile was redefined as 5,280 feet.

One step is the distance one walks when measuring from one foot to the other. A pace or stride, on the other hand is equivalent to every two steps, or the distance between where one foot strikes the ground and where the same foot strikes the ground again.

Measuring your pace or stride is sometimes referred to as finding your "tally". To find your tally, you will need to set up a course in your local terrain and practice. Use a long piece of string and measuring tape to set up a meandering route in the woods of some easily remembered distance such as 100 meters or 100 feet. It is important not to use a straight-line course because your stride will need to naturally adjust for low branches, thick underbrush, and other natural obstacles. Walk the round-trip string route several times over several days both ways and keep track of the number of strides it takes to cover the course. Walk the route with your pack in the morning while you are still energetic, and then also walk the route with your pack in the late afternoon after several hours of hiking or other physical exercise. Once you have completed the course several times, under several conditions, take the number of paces/strides for each trial and obtain an average. (Add up the total paces/strides and divide the sum by the numbers of trials.) This will be your personal "tally" for determining distances in your terrain. For example, if your course was 100 feet long and it took an average of 20 paces/strides to cover the course, your tally is 20 strides for 100 feet, or five feet per pace/stride.

Keep in mind that paces/strides can vary substantially from one individual to another, so it is important for individuals to know their own personal pace/stride length.

Pace Beads, Ranger Beads, Tally Beads
Military, SAR, and some recreational hikers use "Tally Beads" or "Pace Beads" which are beads on a string for each "Tally Step Index" (total number of Tally Steps for a known distance).

There are two methods to construct tally beads:

- Metric-based
- English-based

Metric Based Pacing Beads (Most-used system)
Four beads are located above the knot and nine beads are located below the knot. The four top beads each represent 1000 meters or 1 kilometer. The nine bottom beads each represent 100 meters.

Each time that you reach your Tally Step Index you pull down or pull up one of the bottom beads to represent 100 meters. After performing this process nine times (900 meters) the next time that you reach your tally step index you would pull up or pull down one of the top beads to represent 1,000 meters or one kilometer. Then start the process over again.

- Upper beads (kilometer) counter: four 1,000-meter (one kilometer) beads
- Lower beads: nine 100-meter (1/10 kilometer) beads

English-based Pacing Beads
The English system works on the statute mile instead of kilometers. The method of use is identical to the method stated above with the Metric Based Pacing Beads; the only difference is measurement kilometer versus mile.

- Upper half-mile counter: six 880-yard (or 1/2 mile) beads
- Lower march counter: seven 110-yard (or 1/16 mile) beads

Coordinate Grid Systems

Unfortunately for mapmakers, the earth is basically a sphere and this makes it hard to represent the map accurately on a flat surface for all but small areas. For example, if you were on a large lake, sitting in a small boat, you would only be able to see about six miles in any direction before the curvature of the earth caused the water to go below the horizon.

There are two coordinate grid systems: Latitude/Longitude and United States National Grid (USNG) similar to Universal Transverse Mercator (UTM).

Latitude/ Longitude
The Equator is at an equal distance from the both the North and South Poles; hence the name, Equator. Latitude lines parallel the Equator around the earth. The Equator is located at zero degrees of latitude. The poles are located 90 degrees North and South latitudes, respectively. Longitude is the distance of a point East or West of the Prime Meridian, designated as 0 degrees of longitude, which runs through the Royal Observatory Greenwich, England. Additional lines of latitude and longitude are assigned numbers accordingly.

Latitude
Latitude is the distance of points north or south of the Equator. They are known as PARALLELS because they are parallel to the earth's Equator. Lines of latitude run east-west but north-south distance is measured between them.

Latitude on a Topo Map
The numbers on the left and right sides of the topographical map are Parallel Lines. The Equator is 0 degrees. The degrees of latitude are measured from 0 degrees to 90 degrees. A line 15 degrees north latitude is 15 degrees above the Equator; a line 65 degrees south latitude is 65 degrees below the Equator. North of Equator is called the Northern Hemisphere. South of Equator is called the Southern Hemisphere. Latitude is read and written first.

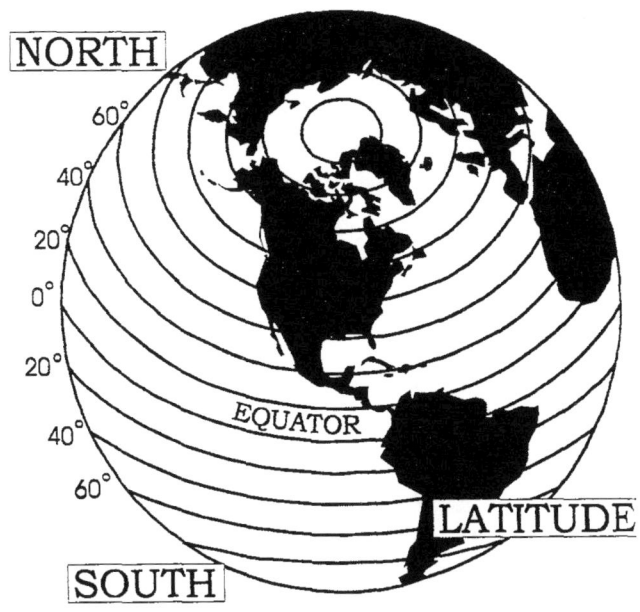

Longitude

The lines of longitude are known as MERIDIANS **and** pass through the North/South Poles at right angles to lines of latitude. Lines of longitude run north-south but east-west distances are measured between them.

Longitude on a Topo Map

The numbers on the top and bottom of the topographical map are Meridian Lines. The Prime Meridian is 0 degrees. The degrees of longitude are measured from 0 degrees to 180 degrees. A line 105 degrees east longitude is 105 degrees counter-clockwise from the Prime Meridian; a line 105 degrees west longitude is 105 degrees clockwise from the Prime Meridian. Longitude is read and written last.

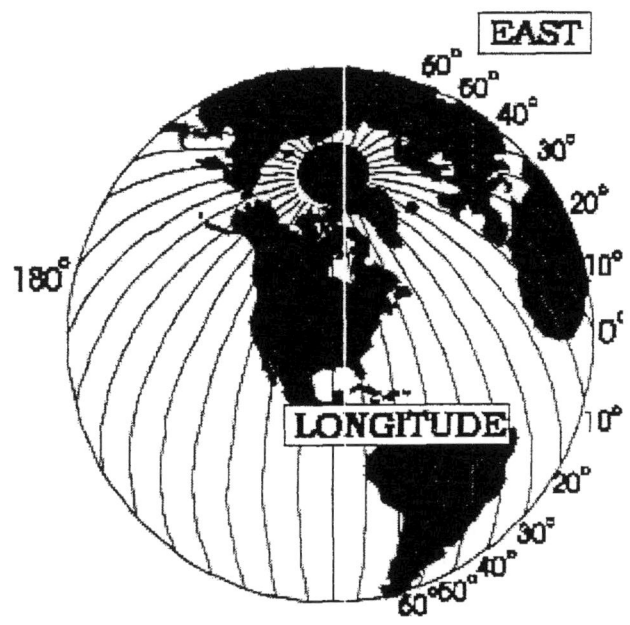

Latitude/Longitude is a geographical coordinate system which coordinates are expressed in angular measurements with a circle divided into 360 degrees, each degree into 60 minutes, and each minute in tenths of a minute. The system is based on distance and time not usually appropriate for foot travel and is difficult to use in the field but is used by pilots and boaters.

Latitude and Longitude should be in one standard format: DD-MM.mmm with latitude being expressed first followed by longitude. Example: 39-35.165 North and 77-16.285 West.

Understanding Latitude and Longitude is important especially in coordinating and communicating from the ground to a search and rescue helicopter or plane.

Universal Transverse Mercator (UTM) and the U.S. National Grid (USNG)

U.S. National Grid System (USNG)
In 2005, the Department of Homeland Security (DHS) recommended the use of a nationally defined coordinate system for all spatial referencing, mapping, and reporting. DHS recognizes that many different coordinate systems can be used to reference incident events in time and space.

The U.S. National Grid is a nonproprietary, alphanumeric referencing system derived from the Military Grid Reference System (MGRS).The objective of this U.S. National Grid standard is to create a more interoperable environment for developing location-based services within the United States and to increase the interoperability of location services appliances with printed map products by establishing a nationally consistent grid reference system as the preferred grid. The U.S. National Grid is based on universally-defined coordinate and grid systems and can, therefore, be easily extended for use worldwide as a universal grid reference system.

USNG relies on the familiar Universal Transverse Mercator (UTM) coordinate system and is applied not only in the United States but also worldwide.

Universal Transverse Mercator (UTM)
Universal Transverse Mercator (UTM) coordinates define two-dimensional, horizontal positions. The 60 UTM zone numbers designate 6-degree-wide longitudinal strips extending from 80 degrees south latitude to 84 degrees north latitude. The zones are numbered 1 through 60 west to east, beginning at 180 degrees west longitude. UTM zone characters are letters which designate eight degree zones extending north and south from the equator. Beginning at 80° south and proceeding northward, 20 bands are lettered C through X, omitting I and O. These bands are all 8° wide except for band X which is 12° wide (between 72–84 N).

Guidelines for Development of UTM

- Be true rectangular grids;
- Have no negative numbers in the coordinates;
- Read left to right and bottom to top;
- Be decimal based; and
- Designed to use the metric system

UTM Grid System

- It can plot points down to ±1 meter.
- Earth is gridded in 1 kilometer quadrants.
- Each kilometer can be broken down to tenths or hundredths.
- Blue tick marks along the edge of the topographic maps are the UTM reference points at one kilometer increments.

Chapter 3 Review Questions

1. Which type of map is preferred for Search and Rescue and why?

_____
_____
_____
_____

2. Describe the following parts of the compass:

   a) _____
   b) _____
   c) _____
   d) _____
   e) _____
   f) _____
   g) _____
   h) _____

3. List the type of compass preferred by in Search and Rescue and why?

_____
_____

4. Universal Transverse Mercator (UTM) and the U.S. National Grid (USNG) is useful because?

_____
_____

5. Define the Tally Step system of measuring distance in the field.

_____

_____

_____

6. List two types of methods used to determine a bearing.

a) _____

b) _____

7. Describe a Nautical chart.

_____

_____

8. Describe a Planimetric map.

_____

_____

9. When using a map for land navigation what five features should the map include?

a) _____

b) _____

c) _____

d) _____

e) _____

10. On 7.5 minute, 1:24,000 scale topographic maps, one inch represents _____ inches or _____ feet.

11. List five methods used to navigate.

a) _____ b) _____

c) _____ d) _____

e) _____

Chapter 4 –

Search and Rescue Resources

Chapter 4   Search and Rescue Resources
- Introduction to the importance of using the right resource in the right place at the right time.
- Human Searchers
- Trackers
- Search Management Teams
- Interviewers and Investigation
- Technical Rescue Teams
- Canine – types, advantages, and disadvantages
- Equestrian/Mounted SAR
- Alzheimer's Association, MedicAlert + Safe Return
- National Center for Missing & Exploited Children – Team Adam
- National Center for Missing Adults
- Emergent (Convergent) Volunteers
- Critical Incident Stress Management (CISM)
- Community Emergency Response Team (CERT)

Upon completion of this chapter and the related course activities, the student will be able to meet the following objectives:

- Identify the various resources used during search incidents.
- List three categories of SAR resources.
- List various SAR canine resources.
- List various organizations that can offer assistance during the search incident.

Chapter 4 – Search and Rescue Resources

This chapter will review the various types of resources used at search and rescue incidents. The focus of this chapter will not only identify the advantages of various SAR resources but also the limitations of each resource. The experienced search manager realizes that SAR resources should be used in a fashion which compliments each other and not to just rely on one resource at a time. An example of relying on one resource is if you were to play an NFL quarterback on the field alone and then after he throws the ball send the receiver onto the field. That sounds absolutely silly. The same is being done when all operations are focused on one resource only, and then an additional resource is brought in only when the outcome of the first resource is not successful.

> *In searching, more people are not necessarily better. Sheer numbers do not guarantee success. Neither does millions of dollars or sophisticated equipment. Even the smallest group of well-trained searchers, under the direction of a skillful search manager or incident commander, is far superior to a large unwieldy group tearing about the country. In fact, the large, untrained, disorganized groups, all too characteristic of searchers done in this country, cost far more lives than they save.*
>
> – Ab Taylor

SAR Resources are separated into three categories which are:
- Human and Animal Resources
- Information Resources
- Equipment and Technology

Search Teams

Hasty Search Teams are usually two- or three-person teams who are highly mobile, well trained, self-sufficient, physically fit, and have good land navigation skills. They utilize fast, non-thorough search tactics in areas most likely to produce clues or the subject themselves. The advantages of Hasty Search Teams are that they can quickly check high probability areas. They can locate clues for use to establish the search area. They can also give an up-to-date assessment and *reconnaissance* of the area including high hazard areas, game trails, etc., in order to update features on maps that may be outdated.

Grid Search Teams use a more systematic approach to searching. Grid Search Teams search in a well-defined, usually small segment. Grid Search has been separated into two disciplines: 1) Loose Grid Search Teams, and 2) Tight Grid Search Teams.

Loose/Open Spaced/Efficient Grid Search Teams have skilled searchers that do not have to stay within eyesight of each other. The larger distance between searchers allows for the use of fewer searchers over a large area. These types of teams often mix voice calls for the subject and whistle-blowing into their visual searches.

Tight/Closed Spaced/Thorough Grid Search Teams search a segment with a confident level of clue detection. The objective of the same group used in evidence searching is to search in a limited, well-defined area for clues. Tight Grid Search Teams are invaluable under the right conditions, but they can be damaging to the environment and clues simply because of each searcher's close proximity to one another. If the tight grid searcher misses the clue the first time, they will probably not get a second chance because they have already destroyed it by stepping on it. Tight Grid Search Teams must be supervised very closely since they may not be as well trained in search techniques. They are usually not self-sufficient and might be more prone to lose their focus on noticing clues and fall back to only looking for the subject.

Human Trackers ("Trackers") search for clues and signs left by the subject. A highly skilled tracker requires a significant amount of training and experience through apprenticeship. Trackers are very efficient and can provide a direction of travel as well as determine areas of high probability. It should be noted that tracker efficiency is decreased significantly once the area has been disturbed by other resources that are less clue-aware. While trackers can be utilized at any time during the SAR incident, the tracker is best applied during the early phase of response. All trained searchers should possess a minimum level of clue consciousness and track awareness.

Search Management is essential in every search incident. Management resources are often among the most important resources to the success of an incident. Search Management Teams analyze the resource needs based on the incident objectives. They determine the strategies needed to achieve the incident objectives and the various tactics required by those strategies. Search Management Teams realize the importance of using multiple different SAR resources at the same time in various areas of the search incident. The benefits of Management Teams are to rationalize actions, determine when to or when not to search or re-search areas. All of these benefits ultimately demonstrate justification of resource allocation, which also may mitigate litigation.

Interviewers and Investigation are vital in every search and rescue incident. Gathering information about the subject is necessary in developing a comprehensive profile on the missing subject. The information gathered will assist in determining the actions needed to locate the subject. While it is always necessary to gather subject information at the beginning of a search, the process should be continuous as the effort progresses. It cannot be expected that the individuals being interviewed are going to be able to answer all of the questions in one sitting (interview). The interviewers should be prepared to perform the interview over the course time. Law enforcement agencies are classically the source for the best investigators. Search and rescue teams are provided training on interviewing family, friends, co-workers, as well as trail and door-to-door interviews in gathering information. An ideal situation would be for the interview to include a law enforcement officer and a trained search manager. Interviewees will tend to recall or describe only a portion of what they know, saw, or heard. This is normal behavior. That is why multiple interviews with multiple interviewers are necessary.

Technical Rope Rescue

Technical Rope Rescue Teams are trained to operate in hazardous terrain consisting of various angles such as low, steep, and high angle. Technical Rope Rescue Teams are very skilled in use of litter evacuation. They can be very useful in gaining safe access with a focus on fall protection. These teams can safely evacuate subjects using technical rope skills on a more direct route rather than having a large number of resources carry the subject a great distance.

New York, NY, September 21, 2001 -- An Urban Search and Rescue crew member from Washington state searches through the rubble for survivors following the terrorist attacks on the World Trade Center.
Photo by Michael Rieger/ **FEMA News Photo**

Urban Search and Rescue (USAR) involves the location, rescue (extrication), and initial medical stabilization of victims trapped in void spaces in debris. Structural collapse is most often the cause of victims being trapped, but victims may also be trapped in transportation accidents, mines, and collapsed trenches.

Urban search and rescue is considered a "multi-hazard" discipline, as it may be needed for a variety of emergencies or disasters, including earthquakes, hurricanes, typhoons, storms and tornadoes, floods, dam failures, technological accidents, terrorist activities, and hazardous materials releases. The events may be slow in developing, as in the case of hurricanes, or sudden, as in the case of earthquakes.

The **Mountain Rescue Association (MRA)** was established in 1959 at Timberline Lodge at Mount Hood, Oregon, making it the oldest Search and Rescue association in the United States.

With over 90 government authorized units in the U.S., Canada and other countries, the MRA has grown to become the critical mountain search and rescue resource in the United States.

The large majority of MRA membership is made up of unpaid professional volunteers who have been fully accredited in Mountain Search and Rescue operations. The remainder of our member teams are "Ex-officio" units, which are paid professionals in governmental service, and "Associate" units which are other mountain SAR-related teams or groups

The Mountain Rescue Association (MRA) is comprised of highly-skilled, active mountain rescue teams from around the country, and has stringent requirements for membership. The teams themselves make up the association; therefore, individual memberships are NOT available.

To become accredited by MRA, each regular member team must pass three different tests based on guidelines drawn up by the association. These tests are conducted on appropriate terrain by at least three current MRA teams working together to evaluate the applicant group being tested. The tests involve high-angle rescue (rock rescue), ice and snow, and wilderness search.

Once a team has achieved full MRA status, it is expected that the new members will be trained to MRA guidelines and tested accordingly by their team. MRA-qualified personnel within teams are called Rescue Members. Accredited teams must re-test every five years to maintain their accreditation in the Mountain Rescue Association.

Because MRA teams are test-qualified by their peers, local, state, and federal agencies feel confident about working with them on search and rescue operations.

Water Rescue

Water rescue has a number of different areas of specialty:
- Tidal
- Lakes
- Swift-water

Swift-water rescue is one of the most dangerous disciplines in technical rescue. This is mostly due to the water's deception. Most people do not realize the true power of moving water. It does not take a high level of water to knock a person off their feet and sweep them downstream. All swift-water rescuers should have the knowledge and skills to read rivers and understand hydrology so that they can interpret water surface conditions indicating underwater obstacles/hazards. Water rescue teams are very familiar with personal flotation devices, water rescue personal safety items, water rescue throw lines, and self-rescue techniques. These teams are a great resource to have if the search area contains large bodies of water or rivers that are prone to flooding.

Canine

Throughout history, dogs have played an important role in man's daily life because of their outstanding scenting abilities. The human nose has approximately five million olfactory cells, and the dog's nose has approximately 220 million. It is estimated that one-eighth of the dog's brain is committed to olfaction.

During both world wars, dogs were used to locate injured soldiers on the battlefield. Often, an injured soldier would crawl away and hide. The dogs were taught to find the injured soldier and return to the handler, who would then follow the dog back to the victim. In World War II, these dogs were called "casualty dogs," and worked with the Medical Corps. Dogs were also trained to detect mines and act as messengers, scouts, trackers, and sentries. The casualty dog was the start of the modern day Search and Rescue dog, taught to locate people who are injured or lost. The search dog has evolved into a specialized tool. (Taken from *Evolution of the Historical Human Remains Detection Dog – Choosing the Best Resource* by Adela Morris and Donna Randolph, *Institute for Canine Forensics Paper* presented at the Society for Historical Archaeology annual conference Sacramento, CA, January 11–15, 2006.)

> Compare the canine"s nose inside to the human nose – it is much longer. The olfactory lobe of the canine is many times larger. Therefore, his brain's ability to register different smells is many times greater than ours. There are different nerves inside of the nose that register smell.
>
> One particular gland (running the long way on the roof of the canine's mouth, like a pancake) is affected by anything that may happen to the large canine teeth. An infected canine tooth will seemingly impair the canine's ability to smell. This makes it doubly important that the canine's mouth be kept healthy. You must pay very close attention to the canine's teeth because these scenting glands are so close to the large canine teeth.
>
> There are many more "scenting cells" within the canine's nose (cross-section) than there are in a human nose. Any scent that travels up the canine's nose goes to all these "sensors" or scenting cells, and fits into the proper "scenting cell" for that particular scent molecule.
>
> There are basically eight different chemical compounds in perspiration. There are five different kinds of bacteria that generally inhabit the human body at all times. What you have, then, is a combination of these eight chemical compounds and five kinds of bacteria comprising odor. As you can see, you can come up with a figure equaling 5,565 different smells. By mixing the different chemical compounds, such as when you are afraid or guilty or whatever, you can emit different odors for each. This is why different people give off different odors when frightened, etc.

> The rafts, airborne with bacteria and sweat on them, still floating around in the air, picked up by the canine, are what is called "air" or "airborne" scent. The canine has his nose lifted in the air and he is really searching those wind currents. If the rafts come to rest on the ground, it is what we call "ground scent". There is, unfortunately, some slight confusion in what is called a "tracking" canine and what is called a "trailing" canine. If some of the rafts have come to rest on the ground, they are going to be some distance away from the person's track, depending on the wind.
>
> There is also the track left as the person steps on the ground, crushing and killing any plants there. When the plant is broken and crushed they excrete different fluids. As these fluids are released by the crushed plant, they interact with bacteria in the soil. Decay (soil bacteria working on the crushed matter) starts immediately. Therefore, footsteps in the above situation would smell differently from an odor produced by perspiration and bacteria.
>
> Information from: Bill Syrotuk - *Scent and the Scenting Dog*

Air Scent Canines detect the scent of "human rafts" (dead human skin cells) as they float through the air. Air scent dogs generally do not discriminate from one scent generator to another. These dogs are usually worked off lead. Air scent dogs are extremely useful in covering large areas, especially if no one has been in those areas. Since the dog is not on lead, it is able to run freely until it locates a scent and follow the scent cone to the scent generator. This process requires that the canine be completely non-aggressive to subjects,  particularly children. This process covers a large area in an extremely efficient amount of time. Weather conditions such as wind and temperature play a large influence when using air scent canine. A small number of air scent canines are further trained to discriminate one scent generator from another. They are very valuable because they can work in the same area as other SAR resources.

Tracking Canines are trained to follow a specific scent matching that of the scent generator, such as from an article of clothing, bed sheets or pillowcases, etc. Tracking canines work on lead, and follow very closely on the trail of where the subject traveled, regardless of wind. They have been known to work very old tracks, some being multiple days old.

www.ssdk9.com

Police Canines are sometimes known as "tracking" and "sniff and bite" dogs. These dogs are trained for law enforcement and military use. Some will track criminal suspect footsteps based on crushed vegetation or the suspect's adrenaline scent. These dogs are also trained to protect their handler from any aggressive action by attacking and biting the aggressor. These dogs work both on and off leash. Because of their trained aggressive behavior they may not be always suitable for missing person searches, especially in the urban environment.

From *Urban Search Managing Missing Person Searches in the Urban Environment*, C. Young and J. Wehbring, dbs 2007

Trailing Canines are said to use both tracking and air scenting techniques. Trailing canines detect the scent of the subject above the ground. Some handlers believe that in certain environments such as urban settings, that a trailing canine off lead may have advantages, whereas some may believe that a tracking canine should be used.

www.absarokasearchdogs.org

Human Remains Detection Canines are used to alert on the specific scent of human remains, including those buried.

ask.afpc.randolph.af.mil/pubaffairs/release/2006/08/Images/060731-F-0123B-016

Disaster Canines are usually air scent discriminating dogs that are trained to alert upon detecting human scent in debris such as collapsed buildings, flooded areas, hurricanes, etc. These dogs are also trained to switch from looking for live finds to those deceased.

Avalanche Canines, similar to disaster canines, are trained to search the areas involved after an avalanche has occurred. They will usually alert and try to dig a hole at the location with the strongest scent.

http://www.bigmtnbelgians.com/brenneravi2.jpg

Water Search Canines will detect the scent and decomposition by-products as they rise to the water surface. Water search dogs can work along the shoreline or on boats.

White Deer Search and Rescue

Equestrian Search and Rescue Teams

Mounted Search Teams have been very useful during searches when used properly. Horses are able to provide the searcher with a much higher platform to search. If the rider has a good ability to read their horse, it has been said that they can notice clues simply by watching the horse move its ears. It has also been said that horses become very skittish when they are near something that has died. The major disadvantage with mounted search team is the destruction that the horse leaves on the area. Since horses are able to carry large loads for a long distance, they are valuable in transporting supplies in rough terrain. The mounted SAR team can also be deployed to establish attraction locations and lookout points and rapidly check all trails.

Alzheimer's Association

The Alzheimer's Association is the leading voluntary health organization in Alzheimer care, support and research. The Alzheimer's Association provides support for those diagnosed with Alzheimer's disease.

One of the important services that the Alzheimer's Association offers is the MedicAlert + Safe Return program.

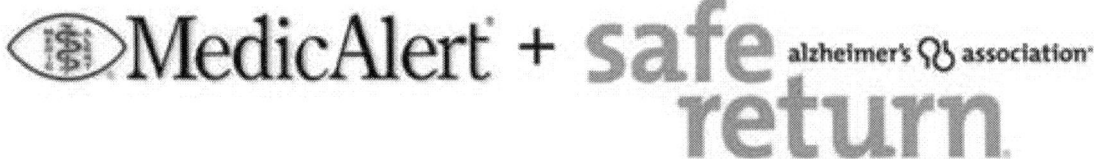

Live 24-hour emergency response service for wandering and medical emergencies

How MedicAlert + Safe Return Works

When a person with dementia wanders or becomes lost, one call immediately activates a community support network to help reunite the lost person with his or her caregiver. When a person is found, a citizen or law official calls the toll-free 24-hour emergency response number on the identification product and the individual's family or caregivers are contacted. The nearest Alzheimer's Association office provides support during search and rescue efforts. In addition, should medical attention be required, access to a personal health record is immediately available. (www.alz.org/index.asp)

National Center for Missing and Exploited Children – Team Adam

Team Adam provides rapid, on-site assistance to law enforcement agencies and families in cases of missing, abducted, and exploited children. Its members are retired law-enforcement professionals with years of investigative experience at the federal, state, and local level.

Team Adam Consultants (TAC) rapidly deploy to sites where cases are unfolding, providing on-the-ground technical assistance and connecting local law enforcement with a national network of resources. Most of the TACs are retired Law Enforcement personnel.

Team Adam's unique access to NCMEC resources, coupled with their years of command post and multi-jurisdictional law enforcement experience, very often provides small- or medium-sized departments with the tools they need to handle complex, media-intensive cases.

The National Center for Missing Adults

The National Center for Missing Adults (NCMA) is a division of Nation's Missing Children Organization, Inc. (NMCO) – a 501c(3) non-profit organization working in cooperation with the U.S. Department of Justice's Bureau of Justice Assistance, Office of Justice Programs.

The National Center for Missing Adults (NCMA) was formally established after the passage of Kristen's Law (H.R. 2780) by the 106th United States Congress on October 26th, 2000. NCMA operates as the national clearinghouse for missing adults, providing services and coordination between various government agencies, law enforcement, media, and most importantly – the families of missing adults. NCMA also maintains a national database of missing adults determined to be "endangered" or otherwise at-risk. More precisely, – NCMA performs the following core legally mandated functions:

- Establish and maintain a national clearinghouse for missing adults.
- Assist law enforcement and families in locating missing adults.
- Serve as a national repository of information accessible to the general public, advocacy groups, and law enforcement for the purpose of tracking missing adults who are determined by law enforcement to be endangered due to age, diminished mental capacity, or the circumstances of disappearance are suspicious, when foul play is suspected or circumstances are unknown.
- Maintain statistical information of adults reported as missing.
- Provide informational resources and referrals to families of missing adults.
- Assist in public notification and provide victim advocacy related to missing adults.
- Develop and deliver training to improve law enforcement response to missing adults and their families through training and promotion of best practices in service delivery.

Emergent (Convergent) Volunteers

Citizens with a desire to help, but with no specialized training, are referred to as emergent, convergent, or spontaneous volunteers. These individuals can be helpful at search incidents if utilized properly. Television and movies commonly demonstrate search tactics using emergent volunteers shoulder to shoulder screaming out the subject's name. Notice that for majority of times they have no personal protective clothing, survival equipment, or knowledge. Emergent volunteers can be helpful in assisting law enforcement, firefighters, and SAR teams with road blocks, handing out flyers, door-to-door notification in urban environments, and providing support and assistance at the Incident Command Post. It is wise for the authority that is ultimately responsible for the incident, which is law enforcement, to verify their identification and perform a criminal check prior to allowing them to participate at the incident site.

Critical Incident Stress Management Teams (CISM)

Critical Incident Stress refers to a stress reaction experienced by emergency responders, which may have debilitating psychological and physiological effects upon them. The stress can be to a single, highly traumatic SAR incident, or to a series of incidents with less impact experienced over a period of time – even years.

There are hundreds of CISM teams in the United States that are comprised of mental health care professionals, trained emergency services personnel, peer counselors and clergy who provide an opportunity for responders to debrief and defuse. Searchers may be exposed to numerous stressful incidents over long periods of time. These multiple exposures can accumulate which can lead to longlasting debilitating effects. Searchers need to be aware of these effects before they become serious.

Community Emergency Response Teams (CERT)

The Community Emergency Response Team (CERT) Program educates people about disaster preparedness for hazards that may impact their neighborhood or workplace and trains them in basic disaster response skills, such as fire safety, light structural search and rescue, team organization, and disaster medical operations. Using the training learned in the classroom and during exercises, CERT members can assist others in their neighborhood or workplace following an event when professional responders are not immediately available to help. CERT members also are encouraged to support emergency response agencies by taking a more active role in emergency preparedness projects in their community. CERT teams are typically associated with the municipal police department or Office of Emergency Management, so they are already aware of their neighborhood, have a general awareness of personal safety, and a minimum level of personal protective equipment. CERT Teams can be very helpful at search incidents. Most have had some level of identity/background check.

Other miscellaneous resources that can be utilized at search and rescue incidents are:

- Fixed-wing aircraft
- Salvation Army
- All-Terrain Vehicles
- Meteorologist
- Avalanche Rescue Teams
- Confined Space Rescue Teams
- Forward Looking Infra-red (FLIR)
- Sonar
- Sound and Vibration Devices
- American Red Cross
- Helicopters
- HAM Operators
- Hazardous Materials Teams
- Cave Rescue Teams
- Mine Rescue Teams
- Thermal Imaging Devices
- Avalanche Beacons
- GPS Devices

> In summation, it is important to understand that all of these resources can be used simultaneously at the search incident. By using the right tool, at the right time, in the right way, you are being the most efficient and productive as possible. Don't rely simply on technology in search activities; keep in mind that the best computer out there is the human brain!

Chapter 4 Review Questions

1. List the three types of resource categories.

   a) _____

   b) _____

   c) _____

2. Describe Loose Spaced Grid Search resources.

   _____
   _____
   _____
   _____

3. Describe the differences between an Air Scent dog and a Tracking dog.

   _____
   _____
   _____
   _____

4. What organization sponsors the "Safe Return" program and what does it consist of?

   _____
   _____
   _____
   _____

5. What is Team Adam?

   _____
   _____
   _____
   _____

6. What is the CERT program?

_____
_____
_____
_____

7. A resource that analyzes the resource needs based on the incident objectives is:

_____
_____

8. Three areas of water rescue include:
a) _____
b) _____
c) _____

9. What is a CISM and why is it considered a valuable resource?

_____
_____
_____
_____

Using the Aguinaldo Search Scenario
- What types of resources should be requested for initial response to this incident?
- How should you employ these resources?

Aguinaldo Scenario

Mr. Magtanggol Aguinaldo is an 87-year-old male who was visiting with relatives for a funeral. Mr. Aguinaldo's wife called 911 after they could not locate him this morning. The first arriving patrol car arrived at 12:30 hours.

Mrs. Aguinaldo informs the police officer that they are from Bacolod, Philippines and that her husband has diabetes and dementia. She last saw him sitting on the front porch of her nephew's home. She said that she went inside to take a nap and when she returned he was no longer there.

Mr. Aguinaldo has the following physical description:
    Light skin black male
    5'10", 180 lbs
    Hazel eyes
    Short black hair
    Clean shaven

Mr. Aguinaldo was last seen wearing:
    Black golf shirt with short sleeves
    Khaki pants
    Brown shoes

Mr. Aguinaldo past medical history:
    Alzheimer's Disease
    Osteoporosis
    Rheumatoid Arthritis
    Angina Pectoris

Mr. Aguinaldo takes the following medication:
    Glipizide 40mg once a day
    Nateglinide 120mg per meal
    Naprosyn 375 mg
    Nitroglycerin 0.4mg

Mr. Aguinaldo speaks English with an accent, Tagalog and some Spanish. Mr. Aguinaldo has had a similair incident once before approximately two years ago when they were on vacation on Margarita Island in Venezuela, but he was found shortly afterwards.

Mr. Aguinaldo did not mention anything out of the ordinary to his wife. Mr. Aguinaldo is not familiar with the area since this is his first visit. The closest relative lives in a neighboring municipality approximately 12 miles away.

Chapter 5 –

Search Philosophy

Chapter 5　　　　　Search Philosophy
- Introduction to Search Theory
  - The "Crucials" of Search and Rescue
- Search Theory Terminology
  - Point Last Seen
  - Last Known Point
  - Probability of Area
  - Probability of Detection
  - Initial Planning Point
- Search Urgency
- Theoretical Search Area
- An overview of Searcher Effectiveness

Upon completion of this chapter and the related course activities, the student will be able to meet the following objectives:

- Have a basic understanding of Search Theory.
- Familiarity with the "Crucials" of Search and Rescue
- Define PLS, LKP, and IPP
- Understand the equation POS = POA x POD
- Understand Search Urgency

Chapter 5 – Search Philosophy

Introduction to Search Theory

Most people do not view search activities as an emergency until a significant amount of time has passed since the subject left, the subject is very young or very old, or the subject has a medical history or problem, all of which are referred to as an "at risk" missing person. This has always been a historical dilemma because to some level a percentage of these subjects do return on their own. Waiting for that possible scenario certainly allows the subject who is not able to return on their own to move farther from their last known point or become more susceptible to the environment. This delay in response is detrimental to the possibility of a successful outcome. This data can be proven simply with the realization that every moment that the subject is able to walk, significant geographical property is addedto the search area.

The **Theoretical Search Area** is the distance that the subject could have traveled in the time elapsed.

In order to minimize the Theoretical Search Area, we need to recognize the seven crucial elements of search and rescue.

Rudiments of Search Management: The "Crucials" of Search and Rescue

- Search is an Emergency
- Maximize the Probability of Success in the Minimum Amount of Time with the Right Resources
- Search is a Classical Mystery
- Search for Clues and the Subject
- Focus on Aspects Important to Success
- Know if the Subject Leaves the Search Area
- Use Tight Grid Search as a Last Resort

The "Crucials" of Search and Rescue

Search is an Emergency

The first problem that is faced with the search incident is how to determine if the subject is indeed in need of rescue and if so, to what level of response is required? Our first mind-set must be to realize that search is an emergency for the following reasons:

- The subject may be in need of medical care either due to an underlying medical condition, injury, or environment.
- The subject may not be properly equipped or trained for the environment
- Time and weather destroys clues

Now back to the question that was raised earlier: once it is determined that a response is necessary, what level of response will it be? A Search Urgency Form is beneficial in this process since it is based on a number of behavioral profile categories including climbers, hunters, fishermen, children, dementia patients, etc. Each question has an answer varying from 1 to 3. The total accumulative number gives you an objective perspective on the type of response. These values certainly are just a guide and not by any means fixed in concrete. Nonetheless, it offers the search manager a means by which to determine what level of response might be required from an investigation aspect to calling out the cavalry and utilizing all resources available. The Search Urgency Form can also be updated as the incident duration increases. The subject may have left in beautiful weather, but with night approaching and the temperature falling more direct search tactics may be required. We will discuss this further in chapter 8, Search Operations.

[Search Urgency Form – Fig. 5.1]

SEARCH URGENCY FORM

Remember The Lower The Number The More Urgent The Response

RATING

A) NUMBER OF SUBJECTS
- One Person _____ 1
- Two Person (if still together) _____ 2
- Three Person (if still together) _____ 3

B) AGE
- Very Young (10 yrs and under) _____ 1
- Very Old (75 yrs or older) _____ 1
- Other _____ 2-4

C) MEDICAL CONDITION
- Known illness requiring medication _____ 1
- Known or suspected injury or illness _____ 2
- Healthy _____ 3
- Known Fatality _____ 4

D) PHYSICAL CONDITION
- Unfit _____ 1
- Fit _____ 2
- Very Fit _____ 3

E) CLOTHING PROFILE
- Inadequate or insufficient for environment _____ 1
- Adequate for environment _____ 2
- Very Good _____ 3

F) EQUIPMENT PROFILE
- Inadequate for activity/environment _____ 1
- Questionable for environment _____ 2
- Adequate for environment _____ 3
- Very Well Equipped _____ 4

G) SUBJECT EXPERIENCE PROFILE
- Not experienced, not familiar with the area _____ 1
- Not experienced, knows the area _____ 2
- Experienced, not familiar with the area _____ 3
- Experienced, knows the area _____ 4

H) WEATHER PROFILE
- Existing hazardous weather _____ 1
- Predicted hazardous weather (8 hrs. or less) _____ 2
- Predicted hazardous weather (more than 8 hrs.) _____ 3
- No hazardous weather predicted _____ 4

I) TERRAIN & HAZARDS PROFILE
- Known hazardous terrain or other hazards _____ 1
- Difficult terrain _____ 2
- Few hazards _____ 3
- Easy terrain, no known hazards _____ 4

TOTAL: _____

IF ANY OF THE NINE CATEGORIES ARE RATED AS A ONE (**1**), REGARDLESS OF THE TOTAL, THE SEARCH MAY REQUIRE AN *EMERGENCY RESPONSE*.

The total should range from 9 to 33, with 9 being the most URGENT!

9-17 Emergency Response   18-27 Measured Response   28-33 Evaluate & Investigate

Fig 5.1

Maximize the Probability of Success in the Minimum Amount of Time with the Right Resources

Using the right resource at the time in the right place is fundamental to establishing an initial search response. Search Managers and Planners are extremely familiar with this concept. Every searcher needs to embrace this concept since any member of the search team who may not be a trained search manager may arrive on scene and have to establish command. As the complexity of the incident increases, the authority should be delegated to more qualified personnel. The searchers at the single resource level still need to keep this concept in mind when awaiting assignment in order to have trust in the overhead management team. If you happen to be in the Staging Area for a considerable amount of time, don't get annoyed and complain; understand that there is a reason for it. Every task being assigned is helpful in locating the subject and personnel should focus on performing their assignments to the best of their abilities. Do not take the attitude of second guessing the management team. Any perspective that you have will certainly be valuable input during your briefing and debriefing.

Search is a Classical Mystery

Since the actual location of the subject is not known, we need to focus efforts to search for clues along with the subject. The clues will lead searchers to the subject(s). There are always many more clues than subjects. The search can be severely complicated if searchers are not aware of what clues to look for and what resources are able to detect them.

> *"You see, but you do not observe."*
> – Sherlock Holmes

Most untrained searchers are just walking through the area looking for the subject and are oblivious to their surroundings.

Search for Clues and the Subject

As mentioned earlier, the subject cannot move through any area without disturbing it in some manner. Bruised patches of grass, leaving their scent, dropping an article, all of these clues are generated by the subject. The searcher needs to sharpen their searching skills to be more aware of their surroundings and inquire more about what potential clues they should be searching for, generated by the subject and environment.

Focus on Aspects Important to Success

Concentrate energy on efforts under your control. Have a positive mental attitude and focus that attention on yourself, your team, and the task that is assigned. Spending time thinking about what the other groups are doing, why is it taking so long to be assigned, or why you have to carry a 24-hour pack instead of an urban pack is a waste of the energy that will be needed for your assignment.

Know If the Subject Left the Search Area
Confine the search area in an attempt to keep the subject from leaving the area that is being searched. It is a true waste of resources to perform a search in an area that the subject is no longer within. The investigative phase must compliment the search phase in an ongoing cycle until the subject is located. Continuously check places that the subject may go in the event that they walked out on their own ability. Check with friends and employees to find out specific information about the subject. This phase must be done early in the incident and quickly, in order to limit the size of the search segment, for every minute that goes by the search area potential increases.

Use Tight Grid Search as a Last Resort
When you go to the movies or watch TV, this is usually what you will see when a search activity is occurring. This type of search has merit when used properly. Unfortunately, it has become the staple of most search activities based on two primary reasons 1) it offers tasks for an abundant amount of untrained personnel who would like to offer assistance, and 2) these untrained individuals view walking through an area as the same as searching an area. This cannot be further from the truth.

Tight Grid Searching does have its merits: in small, well-defined open areas, a tight grid search is extremely useful in collecting evidence and looking for small clues. The disadvantages of these types of search techniques are that if a clue is missed the likelihood that it will be destroyed is extremely high. It is difficult trying to keep these individuals organized and requires a large number of people to cover a realistic search area. It is a very inefficient use of trained searchers.

Tight Grid Search techniques do have a place in search activities but the decision to utilize this tactic as a first line of attack should be seriously weighed.

Search Theory – A Tool to Help Allocate Resources

Search Theory is a mathematical approach to determining how best to find that which we are searching for. The equation of Search Theory consists of:

$$POS = POA \times POD$$

Now before we start talking about mathematics in search activities, let's look at the above theory. First, we apply this theory in everyday activities, whether we're looking for misplaced keys or items in the grocery store. Second, this theory is only useful as a planning tool **before** the search is conducted; after the area is searched, it is either successful or unsuccessful.

Probability of Area - POA
Probability of Area (POA) is the probability of the subject or a clue being in a search segment. POA is defined as a percentage.

Probability of Detection - POD
Probability of Detection (POD) is the probability of a search object being detected, assuming it is in the segment being searched. Probability of Detection (POD) depends on searcher effectiveness, thoroughness, and quality.

Determining what type of clue we're searching for should determine which sensor (searcher, tracker, canine, etc.) would be best suited for the task in question. We wouldn't want to use a helicopter to try to follow a scent from the subject.

Probability of Success - POS
Probability of Success is what planners and first-arriving searchers should focus on. The Probability of Success is the probability of finding the search object (clue or subject) with a particular search tactic in a particular segment.

In the past, the POD was what everyone focused on and it justifiably does warrant an equal quantity of value along with the POA, but the POS is where everyone should focus their planning attention when determining which resources should be used, in what order, and if they should be used simultaneously.

Last Known Point (LKP) is defined as the last place the subject is verifiably known to have been.

Point Last Seen (PLS) is the location at which someone can confirm that the subject was visually identified.

Initial Planning Point (IPP) is usually located at the first LKP or PLS and will never change or move during the incident. The IPP is considered the starting point at which initial assessment and decisions can be ascertained. Depending upon the identified incident objectives, an Incident Command Post may be required; if so, it may be advantageous not to have it located at the IPP due to the potential of destroying possible clues.

Chapter 5 Review Questions

1. List the "Seven Crucials of Search and Rescue."

a) _____

b) _____

c) _____

d) _____

e) _____

f) _____

g) _____

2. Define the following terms:

Probability of Success - _____
_____

Probability of Detection - _____
_____

Probability of Area - _____
_____

POA x POD = POS - _____
_____

3. What is the Search Urgency Form and why does it provide the searcher with valuable information?

_____
_____
_____
_____
_____

4. What is the LKP and what is its importance?

_____
_____

5. What is the PLS and what is its importance?
_____
_____

6. What is Search Theory?
_____
_____

Chapter 6 –

Clue Consciousness

Chapter 6   Clue Consciousness
- Protecting the scene
  - The importance of not destroying clues
- Number of clues vs. number of subjects
- Clue Awareness
- Clue Orientation
- Lost Person Questionnaire
- Planning Data vs. Searching Data
- Categories of Clues
  - Physical
  - Recorded
  - Testimonial
  - Analytical
- Clue Life Span

Upon completion of this chapter and the related course activities, the student will be able to meet the following objectives:

- Know what it means to be "Clue Aware".
- Understand the difference between a "clue" and "sign".
- Familiarity with Clue Orientation Theory.
- Understand how Planning Data and Search Data are related.
- Explain why it is important to protect the scene.
- List the various categories of clues.
- Understand why clues do not last forever.

Chapter 6 – Clue Consciousness

One of the "crucials" of search and rescue is that we search for clues as well as for the subject. This is simply because there are hundreds, if not thousands of clues and signs left by the subject. It is the tracker's creed not to destroy any clues. It is better to have missed the clue than to have destroyed it.

> Oh, how simple it would have been had I been here before they came like a herd of buffalo and wallowed all over it.
> Here is where the party with lodge keeper came, and they have covered all the tracks for six or eight feet around the body.
> – Sherlock Holmes
> In *The Boscombe Valley Mystery*
>
> (from *Fundamentals of Mantracking*. By Ab Taylor and Don Cooper)

The initial priority of all responders involved in the search incident is to **PROTECT** the Last Known Point (LKP) or Point Last Seen (PLS). That is the search effort's starting point, until told otherwise. It is the only place that is KNOWN to have clues or sign left by the subject.

Did someone travel across this snow field?

Clue – objects or facts that may help solve a problem or a mystery.

Sign – any evidence of change from the natural state that is inflicted on an environment by a person's or animal's passage.

> A walking person leaves sign approximately every 18–20 inches, or over 3,000 times per mile, so catching even a small percentage of it shouldn't be much trouble. The problem lies not in finding sign, but in determining which is relevant and which is not.
>
> (from *Fundamentals of Mantracking*. By Ab Taylor and Don Cooper)

Clue Awareness includes the detailed information that clues may provide to the search effort. Preplanning and training are critical keys for clue awareness. A basic clue awareness level should be acquired long before the searchers are called upon for an actual search. The initial clues gathered should substantiate the level of response to the incident. This awareness level separates the untrained searchers (who may unknowingly trample the subject's footprints); from the trained searchers, who will know how to utilize their clue-awareness skills. They avoid walking over tracks or disturbing other possible clues during the search.

Clue Awareness will make the overall search more efficient and effective.

> **Clue Awareness/Clue Consciousness...**
> ... is having the training and experience to understand:
>
> - The importance of clues to the overall search effort
> - Why we focus search efforts for clues and not specifically the subject
> - Which clues could possibly be found that could be associated with the lost person
> - How, when, and where to search an area
> - How to handle clues once found
> - The importance of searching at night
> - That the lack of clues is also a clue

Clue Orientation

All modern search methods and techniques are "Clue Orientated." Who are you searching for? Each subject has individual characteristics and traits. These behaviors, like phobias, experiences, skills, etc. will point the searchers in a direction by understanding what they need to search for. Any measure of clue detection is based on the unique combination of the following:

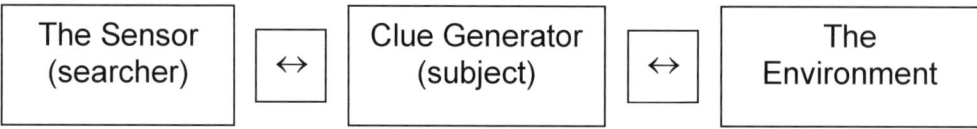

Any change in one of these variables can significantly affect the ease or difficulty of the searcher being able to locate clues.

Clue Orientation Theory is the ability to logically theorize the correlation of a clue to the lost person in a methodical approach. Use of this theory is a learned skill that comes with training and practice.

The **Lost Person Questionnaire (LPQ)** is a multiple page form containing questions that will help obtain information on the lost or missing person in a thorough and logical manner. The Lost Person Questionnaire should be started as soon as possible during the early stage of the search. The information from the LPQ will provide the search managers with details such as what the lost person was wearing; what type of equipment they have with them, if any; their current medical condition; weather conditions; when and where the person was last seen; etc. With this knowledge, search managers will have better insight on the particular clues that might be found.

The detailed information obtained from the LPQ is referred to as "Planning Data" and "Searching Data."

Planning Data	Searching Data
The information that the Planning Section requires in order to plan a strategy for locating the missing or lost person. This may include maps, weather forecast, the subject's trip plans, circumstances of the incident, and relevant lost person statistical behavior data.	The information that searchers require in order to search for the lost subject, such as the subject's name, description, clothing, footwear, and items that the subject may be carrying.

It is important to understand that Search Data is derived from Planning Data. Without substantial information, the planners and searchers have no precise method to justify any strategies.

> **Without Searching Data, it would be like asking searchers to look for a person without any other information. Just search for a person, any person.**

General Clue Categories
Clues may generally be placed into the following categories:

- Physical
- Recorded
- Testimonial
- Analytical

Physical
Any sign or track left on the environment by the subject such as footprints, broken brush or tree limbs, gum/candy/food wrappers, articles that may have been dropped by the subject or human waste.

Recorded
Any documentation left by the subject such as signatures at trail registers, signatures on summit logs, a written itinerary given to family or friends, a route marked on a trail map, or a suicide note.

Testimonial
Clues that are gathered through interviews and investigation are considered testimonials. Interview of witnesses, work colleagues, family, friends, or anyone who may have information about the subject is vital in building a behavioral profile of the

subject. An example of a testimonial clue would be someone providing a PLS. This can be an important clue and it can provide a starting point for the search. Information or details provided by the reporting party could be very important and assist the search effort.

Analytical
Being able to separate things into their constituent parts in order to study or examine them, draw conclusion, and solve problems. Two types of categories exist for Analytical Clues; they are:
- Sensory
- Probable

An example of Sensory clue would be hearing someone call out for help or smelling smoke or human waste.

Probable clues are items found that could very likely be corroborated to the lost subject. This includes clues that could conceivably belong to the lost person, but no information was provided on the LPQ.

An example of a Probable clue would be a small toy found in a search for a missing child. Presently, the clue would be considered probable because it may or may not be the subject's toy; once the toy is identified by the parents, it would become a physical clue.

Clue Life Spans
Clues do not last forever! The searcher must keep in mind that clues age over time and because of weather. Another reason why clues have limited life spans is because animals or people may disturb them.

Weather conditions will certainly play a definitive role in the life span of clues:

Wind – can blow clues from the original location to another. It can cover clues with leaves or other debris. Strong winds can actually mask the sounds of someone calling for help or disperse a scent.

Rain – can flood or destroy tracks and other clues. Like wind, water can move clues from their original locations and move them to another location.

Frost/ice/snow – can highlight or hide clues. Freezing temperatures may also hold the clue for a longer period of time even while aging occurs.

Heat – can obviously melt or evaporate certain clues. The clue may reflect the light to make it easier to see.

Time is a searchers' worst enemy. It will deteriorate and destroy the clue the longer it is exposed to the elements.

Chapter 6 Review Questions

1. Why do searchers prioritize their search attention on clues and not just the subject?
   _____

2. The initial priority of all responders involved in the search incident is to _____ the _____ or _____.

3. Clue Awareness includes -
   _____
   _____

4. The definition of "Sign" is -
   _____
   _____

5. List three variables of clue orientation -
   a) _____
   b) _____
   c) _____

6. List four categories of clues.
   a) _____
   b) _____
   c) _____
   d) _____

7. Examples of factors that affect clue life span?
   _____
   _____

8. Using Clue Orientation Theory, list possible clues that you might search for if searching for two 34-year-old experienced backpackers, who were on a three-day trek using a well-marked trail. Explain briefly why you selected each clue.

_____
_____
_____
_____
_____
_____
_____

9. What is the LPQ and why does it provide the searcher with valuable information?

_____
_____
_____
_____
_____

Using the Aguinaldo Search Scenario
- Identify what information would be considered Planning Data.
- Identify what information would be considered Search Data.
- What various categories of clues have been provided and list them.

Aguinaldo Scenario

Mr. Magtanggol Aguinaldo is an 87-year-old male who was visiting with relatives for a funeral. Mr. Aguinaldo's wife called 911 after they could not locate him this morning. The first arriving patrol car arrived at 12:30 hours.

Mrs. Aguinaldo informs the police officer that they are from Bacolod, Philippines and that her husband has diabetes and dementia. She last saw him sitting on the front porch of her nephew's home. She said that she went inside to take a nap and when she returned he was no longer there.

Mr. Aguinaldo has the following physical description:
    Light skin black male
    5'10", 180 lbs
    Hazel eyes
    Short black hair
    Clean shaven

Mr. Aguinaldo was last seen wearing:
    Black golf shirt with short sleeves
    Khaki pants
    Brown shoes

Mr. Aguinaldo past medical history:
    Alzheimer's Disease
    Osteoporosis
    Rheumatoid Arthritis
    Angina Pectoris

Mr. Aguinaldo takes the following medication:
    Glipizide 40mg once a day
    Nateglinide 120mg per meal
    Naprosyn 375 mg
    Nitroglycerin 0.4mg

Mr. Aguinaldo speaks English with an accent, Tagalog and some Spanish. Mr. Aguinaldo has had a similair incident once before approximately two years ago when they were on vacation on Margarita Island in Venezuela, but he was found shortly afterwards.

Mr. Aguinaldo did not mention anything out of the ordinary to his wife. Mr. Aguinaldo is not familiar with the area since this is his first visit. The closest relative lives in a neighboring municipality approximately 12 miles away.

Chapter 7 –

Search Tactics

Chapter 7   Search Tactics
- An Overview of Initial Search Tactics
- Direct vs. Indirect Tactics

Upon completion of this chapter and the related course activities, the student will be able to meet the following objectives:

- Understand the difference between "direct" and "indirect" tactics.
- Familiarity with a variety of specific direct and indirect tactics.

Chapter 7 – Search Tactics

Overview of Search Tactics

As we have seen, a well-coordinated search is an organized and orchestrated response to a lost-person incident. The total overall outcome of the search may be determined within the first hours of the response. In this chapter, we will discuss the initial tactics that should be implemented when responding to these types of incidents.

Tactics are all the techniques employed to actually find the lost subject or clues and are usually applied by the searchers immediately following first notice. Tactics are important to field personnel because they are the methods by which SAR team members get physically involved with the search function.

There are two categories of search tactics:

- Indirect/Passive Tactics
- Direct/Active Tactics

Indirect Tactics (Passive)

The purpose of Indirect (Passive) Tactics is to bring the subject to the searchers. Indirect tactics (historically referred to as "passive" tactics) do not involve physically entering and moving through the search area to look for the subject or clues. Specific tactics used in this mode include:

- Confinement/Containment
- Investigation
- Attraction

Confinement/Containment

Containment techniques involve efforts to confine the movement of a lost subject in order to minimize the size of the search area. Specific types of containment include:

- Route blocks – trail, road, etc.
- Lookouts – a searcher in a high position overlooking the search area
- Track traps – looking for tracks in areas where tracking is very easy
- Road Patrols

Searchers assigned to containment positions may have to remain at their post for long periods of time. This may require additional logistical support and searchers assigned to such post should not hesitate to request it.

Attraction

Attraction techniques involve calling the subjects attention to searchers. It can range from emergency vehicle lights and loud sounds to the smell of a campfire.

Examples:

Visual:
- Lights
- Aircraft
- Strobes
- Fires
- Beacons
- Flares
- Balloons
- Smoke

Sound:
- Horns
- Voices
- Gunshots
- PA systems
- Sirens
- Whistles

> Note: searchers should not forget to listen for a response from the subject.

Direct Tactics (Active)
The purpose of Direct (Active) Tactics is to bring the searcher to the subject. Direct tactics requires someone to commit resources to actively search for the person. Specific tactics include:

- Hasty Search/Trail running
- Human Trackers
- Trailing Dogs

(Refer to Chapter 4: Search and Rescue Resources for more information)

Investigation/Interview/Information/Intelligence
Investigation is indispensable to the planning staff. The first step in gathering information about the lost person is the Lost Person Questionnaire Form. The data interpreted from this form provides specific information about the lost subject. This is the core of developing an effective search plan. It is essential that a subject profile is developed as early as possible in order for proper and timely allocation of resources to search for the subject. Searchers should become familiar and comfortable with the Lost Person Questionnaire Form (see appendix 7) in order for them to conduct a conversation with the subject's family, friends, and co-workers. It is difficult to establish a connection with people when one is reading and writing on a piece of paper, and only occasionally making eye contact with the person being interviewed. Notice that we are now using the word *interview*. There is a substantial amount of information that a civilian volunteer searcher will not have access to for a number of reasons. The law enforcement agency is ultimately responsible for the missing person. There are advantages and disadvantage to having the law enforcement agency representative present when searchers are interviewing individuals. Sometimes civilian search interviewers can set prospective witnesses more at ease. However, law enforcement interviews can be very effective. A sequence of interviews may reveal a variety of

information, more than the product of one interview. It is important to remember that as a searcher you should not turn an interview into an interrogation.

One subtle but major hindrance during a search is the cessation of information and intelligence during the search. It is extremely difficult to complete the Lost Person Questionnaire in one sitting; it will certainly not be thorough. The Investigation is a critical indirect search tactic since it tells the searchers what that individual subject might do based on their personal characteristics in that given circumstance. Remember, the investigation should occur both initially and throughout the search effort. The lack of proper investigation continues to be a major problem during many search activities throughout the world.

Chapter 7 Review Questions

1. List and describe the two categories of search tactics.

    a) _____

    _____

    b) _____

    _____

2. Give two examples of confinement/containment tactics.

    a) _____

    b) _____

3. Define the following terms.

Attraction - _____

_____

Confinement - _____

_____

4. List two categories of Attraction techniques.

    a) _____

    b) _____

5. List three Direct/Active Search Tactics.

    a) _____

    b) _____

    c) _____

Chapter 8 –

Search Operations

Chapter 8 Search Operations
- Chain of actions upon arrival at the scene
- Anatomy of the Search Effort
- Searcher Consciousness – Responders Attitude, Responsibilities, and Expectations
    - Checking In/Out
    - Proper Briefing/Debriefing
    - Personal Critique

Upon completion of this chapter and the related course activities, the student will be able to meet the following objectives:

- Know what to do when arriving on scene
- Understand the importance of Search Urgency
- General Briefings vs. Tactical Briefings
- The importance of Debriefing
- The value of the Personal Critique

Chapter 8 – Search Operations

Anatomy of the Search Effort

One of the "Crucials" of SAR is that Search is an Emergency! This philosophy is truly acknowledged by responders in the wilderness areas of North America. It is still somewhat of a strange notion in more urban environments. In urban environments, the urgency of the search is based on the subject being "at risk" due to age, health or altered mental status. The younger the subject the more urgent the search and all resources are generally mobilized, while if the elderly walks away they may not get the same level of response. Although age certainly plays one role in determining the urgency of the search, it is by no means the single component. When the initial call is made for the missing subject, the focus must be on interpreting clues from the initial contact. Completing the Search Urgency Form should be performed as early as possible. This urgency rating is not static in nature, it can change over time. However, the Search Urgency Form justifies initial actions such as performing investigation or calling out the search cavalry.

The Search Urgency Form consists of a number of different categories:

1. Age
2. Medical Condition
3. Number of Subjects
4. Subject Experience Profile
5. Weather Profile
6. Equipment Profile
7. Terrain/Hazards Profile

The accumulative numerical value that is determined by the Search Urgency Form will justify the resource allocation. See appendix 6 for a copy of the Search Urgency Form.

Arriving on Scene/Check-In

Upon arriving, even though it may seem trivial, it is important that your whereabouts can be accounted for at all times while you are participating at the incident. There are numerous systems used for resource management and personnel accountability. Regardless of the system used, everyone must check-in as they arrive on the scene.

Generally, you will check in as a single resource, strike team, or task force. The ICS 211 Check-In form (available in appendix 4) is usually used for check-in at incidents. Pertinent information gathered on this form includes:

- Name of agency or organization.
- Whether the resource is a single resource, strike team or a task force.
- The kind of resource.
- The type of resource.
- Name/I.D. Number.

- Date and time resource is checking-in.
- Resource Leader's name, other members' names.
- Number of personnel.
- Whether a manifest is provided.
- Weight of crews or individuals weight.
- Home base and contact information.
- Departure point.
- Method of travel.
- Incident assignment (if known).
- Other qualifications.

This information is necessary for the search manager to able to use resources properly and assure safety for the resources. Ideally, during the check-in process, the searcher will be given information concerning the scheduling of the general and/or tactical briefings.

After check-in, the searcher will have to determine if initial search planning has been set up; if not, the first arriving resource will have to focus on assuring that the ICS for the search incident is begun. The initial search management task will comprise of:

1. Identify the Incident Command Post.
2. Establish a Staging Area with a Check-In.
3. Corroborate and Protect the PLS/LKP.
4. Start the investigative process with the LPQ.
5. Protect any potential scent articles, subject's residence or any other clues.
6. Begin confinement tactics (media, road patrols/blocks, etc.)
7. Identify initial incident objectives and resource need.

If the ICS and search management are already established, then the searcher will have some time to wait for an assignment after checking in. It is wise to use this time to check your pack for items that you will need often such as pad and pencil, compass, etc. Take them out of your pack or move them to convenient parts of your pack.

General and Tactical Briefings

A General Briefing is usually conducted by the Planning Section Chief. It usually includes the major aspects of the search mission, the incident action plan and the incident objectives. It can also include other information such as:

- General situation
- Overall strategies
- Organization of the mission and identification of Command and General Staff members
- Agencies providing resources
- General subject information
- Safety Briefing

Once you have been assigned to a task, you will be given a Tactical Briefing by the IC, Operation Section Chief, or your Crew Leader as to the specific details of your assignment.

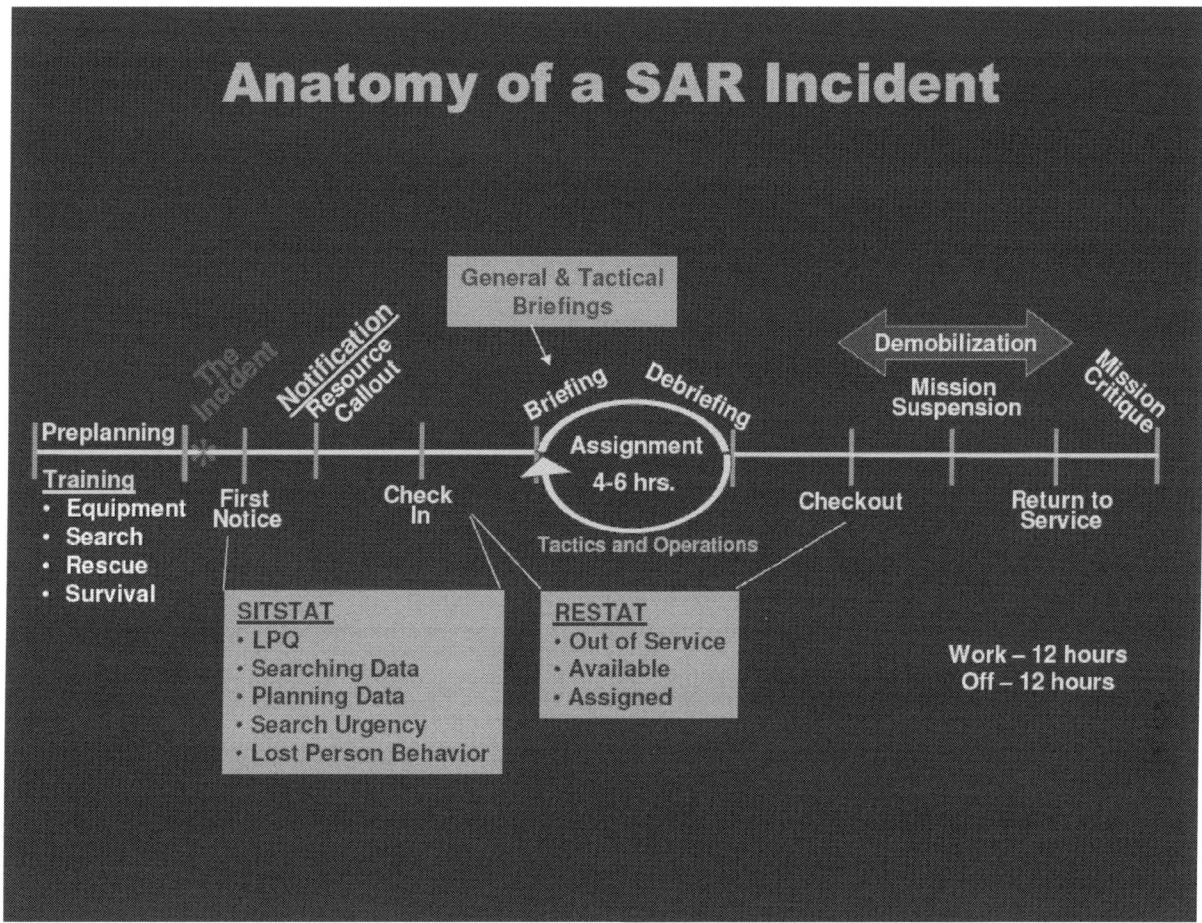

The operational period of a missing person incident.

Searcher Consciousness – Attitude, Responsibilities and Expectations

Searcher attitude starts long before responding to the search mission. It is lifestyle, as a search can occur at any time. This means that the searcher should be physically and mentally fit, be properly prepared for an assignment, and be proficient and competent for the responsibilities that may be asked on the search mission. Moreover, it also means knowing your limitations, your equipment and your team. The safety of yourself, your crewmembers, and the lost subject, to a large extent, depends on how honest and thorough you have been in preparing for the SAR mission.

If you have any doubts about your ability to be an effective and efficient crewmember, either before or during a mission, you should make your crew leader aware of those doubts.

As a searcher, the right attitude regarding the search mission is everything. Searchers should be clue conscious and aware of a basic description of the subject when responding to the incident because they may pass the subject as they are traveling to the scene. Searchers need to maintain a positive mental attitude and demonstrate a willingness to help regardless of the task. This attitude needs to start as soon as the searcher picks up the phone call with the request.

There are numerous functions and activities within the Base, Command Post and various branches that need to be filled. It is important for searchers to realize that filling these positions is vital in the overall effort. The desire to want to stay at the base while others are going into the field may be somewhat difficult to accept; however, the search mission is a balancing act between the planning and operational sections. Always keep in mind that everyone from the local restaurant supplying food for an operational period to the meteorologist giving a weather forecast, EVERYONE makes a meaningful contribution to the search effort.

Debriefing Upon Completion of Assignment

The task assignment debrief occurs when your task reports back in at the Staging Area. It is a vital step in the information flow. The Planning Section will not be able to improve their picture of the incident without quality feedback from field teams. Information such as whether or not the detectability in the field matched what was predicted (POD), likely hitherto unknown hazard areas that might have been discovered, map or trail updates, or any other relevant thoughts and impressions that the team members might have had.

Checking-Out

The check-out procedure is as important as the check-in process. It is critical that you checkout before leaving the incident. If the crew arrived together with a leader, it is an acceptable practice for that leader to sign the crew in and also sign the crew out. It is also acceptable to have each person physically sign themselves in and out. Procedures are likely to vary from agency to agency. Regardless, make sure that you are indeed checked out.

Personal Critique

Many SAR responders carry a small notebook and on the way home or during the first hour's home, they record ways to improve :

- "My headlamp wasn't good on my hat"
- "I could have been better with my navigation skills"
- "I was pleased with my clue-consciousness skills"

The purpose of this is to "evaluate your crew of one" so that you can be better prepared and more effective on the next assignment. There will also be an opportunity to share your thoughts at the Incident Critique (After-Action Report (AAR)) as well.

Chapter 8 Review Questions

1. Why is it important to always establish a check-in at the SAR incident?

   _____

   _____

   _____

2. List and describe two types of briefings.

   a) _____

   _____

   b) _____

   _____

3. Describe why a critique is essential.

   _____

   _____

4. Why is it important for all searchers to always check-out at an incident?

   _____

   _____

5. Searchers need to maintain a _____ and demonstrate a _____ to help regardless the task.

Chapter 9 –

Introduction to Lost-Person Behavior

Chapter 9   Introduction to Lost-Person Behavior
- Who Are We Searching for?
- Why Are We Searching for Them?
- Where Should We Search for Them?
- When Should We Search for Them?
- Search Data vs. Planning Data
- Factors Affecting Lost-Person Behavior
- Categories of Lost Persons
- Preventing the Population at Risk from Becoming Lost

Upon completion of this chapter and the related course activities, the student will be able to meet the following objectives:

- Understand the benefits of being familiar with lost-person behavior.
- Be familiar with the various categories of lost-person profiles.
- Understand the way people react when they become lost.

Chapter 9 – Introduction to Lost-Person Behavior

Who Are We Searching for?

Searchers must be informed about what items they are searching for along with the physical description of the subject. The understanding that the individual person is missing is merely a snapshot of the overall picture of the incident. Each bit of clothing, items that the subject may have and even their scent become essential clues that may lead searchers to the subject. What did the subject have with them when they were last seen? For example, if the subject likes gum, what type and brand? Being able to differentiate the type of gum will reduce a real clue from those that the subject did not prefer.

Lost-Person Behavior provides the search planners with general indications of what the subject may or may not do, such as:

- How far can the subject travel?
- How large should the search area be?
- Where should confinement tactics be used?
- How thoroughly should we search?
- What kind of clues should we be searching for?
- How difficult will it be to detect the subject?
- Will the subject respond or evade?
- When is it time to suspend the search effort?

Search planners use the subject behavioral profile for a number of reasons:

- Determining search strategy
- Defining the search area
- Estimating resource needs
- Mapping the search area
- Briefing search teams

Searchers should try to develop a subject behavioral profile as soon as possible in order to provide two categories of data:

1) Planning Data
2) Search Data

Planning Data

Any information used to develop a strategy for finding the subject. This might include, but is certainly not limited to, the Lost Person Questionnaire Form, maps, present and past events leading up to the incident, statistical and theoretical data, and weather forecasts.

Search Data

Any information that the searchers entering the search areas must be made aware of, in order for them to locate as many clues as possible that belong to the subject being searched for. If this data is correctly examined, it will reduce a significant number of false reports and picking up garbage in the area. The searchers should document all Searching Data during their briefing. Without proper searching data the searchers are just searching for anyone and everyone.

The Search Data List should include, but is not limited to, the following:

Lost Subject's
- Name
- Gender
- Physical description
  - height & weight
  - age
  - build
  - hair color, length, and style
  - facial hair
  - facial features
  - distinguishing marks
  - general appearance

Lost Subject's Clothing
- Kind and type
- Style
- Color
- Size
- Overall detectability
- Footwear
  - size measurement
  - sole type

Lost Subject's Habit/Personality
- Smoke (Y/N) – what, brand, how many times per day
- Alcohol (Y/N) – what, brand, how much
- Drugs (Y/N) – what, brand, how much
- Gum, candy, anything else?

Lost Subject's Health/Condition
- Overall physical condition
- Disabilities
- Medication (Y/N), types, dosage
- Vision – Eyeglasses / Contacts
- Travel aids (cane, walker, etc.)

Lost Subject's Equipment
- Specialty equipment (backpacks, tents, sleeping bags, ground pads, etc.)
- Hunting gear (firearms, archery, etc.)
- Fishing gear
- Camera gear
- Money / Credit Cards

For a more structured view of this data, refer to appendix 7, Lost-Person Questionnaire Form.

Factors Affecting Lost-Person Behavior

General States of Physical and Mental Health – The subject's health may determine the kind and type of clues they may or may not leave. Their general health also plays a considerable factor in determining their survivability.

Personality – The subject's experience plays a significant factor in how they will react in a crisis. If the subject has experience such as camping, military, hunting, or search and rescue they may have the knowledge and skills necessary for survival, thus increasing their chances of survivability even in the most adverse conditions. Subjects that have the "will to live" make a considerable difference between those that live from those that perish under similar conditions.

Outdoor experiences, survival training, and related skills may indicate the kind and number of clues the subject may leave.

Terrain, vegetation, and weather may contribute to how the lost person behaves. Steep elevations, ravines, and bodies of water which we refer to as "natural boundaries" may guide or channel the subject into natural catchments. Some subject categories tend to stay on trails as opposed to others that have a general tendency to leave the trails.

Weather conditions will also play a role in how the subject may respond; for example, during inclement weather conditions most people will seek some form of shelter or cover.

Physiological effects caused by exposure to the environment may cause the subject to leave clues we think no one in their right mind would leave (sleeping bag, pack, water, map, etc.) – the key point here is that they may not be in their right mind.

Standing on the Shoulders of Giants

In the past 30 to 40 years significant studies have been performed which substantially changed the way that we profile missing subjects. People like William Syrotuck, Robert Koester, David Stooksbury, Ken Hill, Don Cooper, and Dennis Kelly along with others developed subject profile categories, methods of determining probabilities of success using quantification, and assessing the searcher's ability to detect clues in various types of terrain and weather conditions.

William Syrotuck wrote *Analysis of Lost Person Behavior: An Aid to Search Planning* in 1976. In his study, Syrotuck analyzed case reports of 229 search incidents occurring mostly in the U.S. states of Washington and New York. He recorded significant behaviors of lost persons, such as the circumstances under which they became lost, whether they traveled up or down in hilly terrain, and features of the environment that contributed to their disorientation.

Syrotuck developed six "lost-person categories" including:

- Small Children (1 to 6 years of age)
- Children (6 to 12 years of age)
- Hunters
- Hikers
- Elderly (over the age of 65)
- Miscellaneous

New information is being developed and included in Robert Koester's newest manual with many more categories.

These materials should always have some influence with Planning Data in modern scientific search management and are addressed in more detail in more advanced training.

How People React to Becoming Lost

Regardless of the subject's age, gender, or experience, at some point when a subject comes to the realization that they are truly lost the first emotions experienced are anxiety and fear.

The mental impact of being lost or disoriented may vary from person to person, but with the exception of one with dementia or Alzheimer's, all experience some level of anxiety. This may lead to emotional and physiological consequences that skew normal thought processes and problem solving. This syndrome can cause catastrophic results for those unaccustomed to these events. How lost subjects handle this sudden onset of emotion plays strongly into their survivability and likelihood of being found sooner rather than later.

Preventing the Population at Risk from Becoming Lost

By being familiar with this statistical data, search teams can identify certain categories as individuals at high risk of becoming lost if the opportunity avails itself. For example, measures should be instituted at nursing homes, assisted living residence and senior citizens centers for those with residents with dementia and Alzheimer's to reduce the occurrence of walk-aways. These measures should also include the actions that should take place in the event that someone does walk-a-way (i.e., recent digital photo, emergency contact information). Some patients/residents have been equipped with tracking devices.

Preventative search and rescue programs including "Hug-a-Tree", "Lost...But Found Safe and Sound", and "Lost in the Woods" all provide information for children and parents on how to stay safe in the wilderness setting and if they become separated and lost, what they should do until found.

Chapter 9 Review Questions

1. List four reasons why knowledge of lost person behavior can be an advantage to the searcher.
   a) _____
   b) _____
   c) _____
   d) _____

2. List four factors of lost person behavior we should consider.
   a) _____
   b) _____
   c) _____
   d) _____

3. Why is searching data so important to searchers?
   _____
   _____

4. List five categories of lost person behavior.
   a) _____
   b) _____
   c) _____
   d) _____
   e) _____

5. Describe how people react to becoming lost.
   _____
   _____

6. Who wrote *Analysis of Lost Person Behavior: An Aid to Search Planning*?
   _____

Using the Aguinaldo Search Scenario
- Which statistical behavioral profile does the subject fall under?
- Based on the statistical data what is the detectability of the subject?
- How would indirect tactics best be used in this incident?

Aguinaldo Scenario

Mr. Magtanggol Aguinaldo is an 87-year-old male who was visiting with relatives for a funeral. Mr. Aguinaldo's wife called 911 after they could not locate him this morning. The first arriving patrol car arrived at 12:30 hours.

Mrs. Aguinaldo informs the police officer that they are from Bacolod, Philippines and that her husband has diabetes and dementia. She last saw him sitting on the front porch of her nephew's home. She said that she went inside to take a nap and when she returned he was no longer there.

Mr. Aguinaldo has the following physical description:
    Light skin black male
    5'10", 180 lbs
    Hazel eyes
    Short black hair
    Clean shaven

Mr. Aguinaldo was last seen wearing:
    Black golf shirt with short sleeves
    Khaki pants
    Brown shoes

Mr. Aguinaldo past medical history:
    Alzheimer's Disease
    Osteoporosis
    Rheumatoid Arthritis
    Angina Pectoris

Mr. Aguinaldo takes the following medication:
    Glipizide 40mg once a day
    Nateglinide 120mg per meal
    Naprosyn 375 mg
    Nitroglycerin 0.4mg

Mr. Aguinaldo speaks English with an accent, Tagalog and some Spanish. Mr. Aguinaldo has had a similair incident once before approximately two years ago when they were on vacation on Margarita Island in Venezuela, but he was found shortly afterwards.

Mr. Aguinaldo did not mention anything out of the ordinary to his wife. Mr. Aguinaldo is not familiar with the area since this is his first visit. The closest relative lives in a neighboring municipality approximately 12 miles away.

Chapter 10 –

Getting Involved

Chapter 10   Getting Involved
- Laying the Foundation in Forming a SAR Team
- Resources Available to Help Start a Team
    - NASAR
    - American Red Cross
    - State SAR Councils

Upon completion of this chapter and the related course activities, the student will be able to meet the following objectives:

- Understand where and how to get information on finding and/or building a Search and Rescue team.

Chapter 10 – Getting Involved

Laying the Foundation in Forming a SAR Team

The basis for the creation of any search and rescue team is a need for service. Most teams form simply because of: 1) individuals with similar interest and desire to help others or 2) one or more SAR incidents have occurred and an absence of trained resources have been recognized. Regardless of the reason, all SAR groups have a commonality of the inherent motivation to help those in need. There is little glory and fame for those who participate in search and rescue.

When considering forming a search and rescue team, the first step that should be taken is to research if there is a SAR group in the area. Many states have created state SAR Councils, Associations, or Federations that consist of SAR teams throughout that particular state. It is well worth the time and effort to contact these groups

Resources Available to Help Start a Team

National Association for Search and Rescue (NASAR)

The National Association for Search and Rescue, Inc. (NASAR) is a not-for-profit membership association dedicated to advancing professional, literary, and scientific knowledge in fields related to search and rescue. NASAR is comprised of thousands of paid and non-paid professionals interested in all aspects of search and rescue – the humanitarian cause of saving lives – throughout the United States and around the world. "...that others may live."

Response to persons in distress has long been an honorable, charitable tradition. The professionals in search and rescue have carried on this tradition of helping others by dedicating time, information, skills, equipment, and funding to the relief of suffering. NASAR actively works toward the development of improved coordination and communications among federal, state, local, and volunteer groups. NASAR's primary goal is to develop and provide professional credentialing products and services for the search and rescue community.

American Red Cross

For more than 125 years, the mission of the American Red Cross has been to help Americans prevent, prepare for and respond to emergencies. They have a long and proven track record of immediate response to major disasters, both natural and human-caused.

Disasters deprive families of homes and belongings, cause major disruptions to businesses and cost billions. This immense social and economic impact can be dramatically reduced if families, businesses and communities take proactive steps to reduce their vulnerabilities. Therefore, disaster preparedness and mitigation are top priorities of the American Red Cross.

The American Red Cross has joined forces with the Department of Homeland Security, Federal Emergency Management Agency (FEMA), the insurance industry, emergency management and environment officials, educators, businesses and other partners who are concerned about the increasing, and often unnecessary, losses caused by disasters. Across the nation, they are working to build a "culture of preparedness" and to limit the harm inflicted on families and communities by disasters. The Red Cross has three primary roles in community disaster preparedness and mitigation: awareness and education, direct mitigation, and advocacy.

State SAR Councils
(These State SAR Agencies are current at time of print.)

Alaska Search and Rescue Association
Appalachian Search and Rescue Conference
Arizona Search and Rescue Council
Arkansas State SAR Association
Bay Area Search and Rescue Council
Colorado Search and Rescue State Advisory Council
Florida Association for Search and Rescue
Idaho State Search and Rescue
Indiana Search and Rescue Association
Kentucky Search and Rescue
Maine Association for Search and Rescue
Maryland Search Teams Task Force
New Jersey Search and Rescue Council
New Mexico Search and Rescue Council
New York Federation of Search and Rescue Teams
North Carolina Search and Rescue Advisory Council
Oregon State Search and Rescue Advisory Committee
Pennsylvania Search and Rescue Council
Washington Search and Rescue Volunteer Advisory Council
West Virginia Search and Rescue Network
Wyoming Search and Rescue Council

References

Alzheimer's Association. Safe Return®.
http://www.alz.org/we_can_help_safe_return.asp

Cooper, Donald C., Patrick (Rick) LaValla, and Robert (Skip) Stoffel. 1999. *Search and Rescue Fundamentals: Basic skills and knowledge to perform wilderness, inland, search and rescue,* 3rd ed., revised. Tacoma, WA: ERI International.

Hill, Kenneth A. *Lost Person Behavior.* 1997. Ottawa: National SAR Secretariat.

Hill, Kenneth A. *Managing the Lost Person Incidents.* 2nd Ed., 2007 Chantilly, VA: National Association for Search and Rescue.

Kelley, Dennis. *Mountain Search for the Lost Victim.* California. 3rd Printing 1987.

National Wildfire Coordinating Group (NWCG). *The Incident Command System National Training Curriculum,* Developed by the Interagency Steering Group. Boise, ID: National Interagency Fire Center, Division of Training 1994.

Setnicka, Tim. *Wilderness Search and Rescue.* K. Andrasko, Ed. Boston MA: Appalachian Mountain Club, 1980.

Taylor, Albert (Ab) and Donald Cooper. *Fundamentals of Mantracking: The Step-By-Step Method.* 2nd Ed., Olympia, WA: Emergency Response Institute and National Rescue Consultants, 1997.

Young, Christopher and John Wehbring. 2007. *Urban Search: Managing Missing Person Searches in the Urban Environment.* Virginia: dbS Production 2007.

Appendices

Appendix 1 - Incident Command System Incident Briefing 201 Form

Appendix 2 – Incident Command System Assignment List 204 Form

Appendix 3 – Incident Command System Medical Plan 206 Form

Appendix 4 – Incident Command System Check-In 211 Form

Appendix 5 – Incident Search Urgency Form

Appendix 6 – Lost Person Questionnaire Form

Appendix 7 – Incident Command System 214 Form – Unit Log

Appendix 1 - Incident Command System Incident Briefing 201 Form

INCIDENT BRIEFING	1. INCIDENT NAME	2. DATE PREPARED	3. TIME PREPARED
	4. MAP SKETCH		

ICS 201 (12/93) NFES 1325	PAGE 1	5. PREPARED BY (NAME AND POSITION)

6. SUMMARY OF CURRENT ACTIONS

ICS 201 (12/93)
NFES 1325 PAGE 2

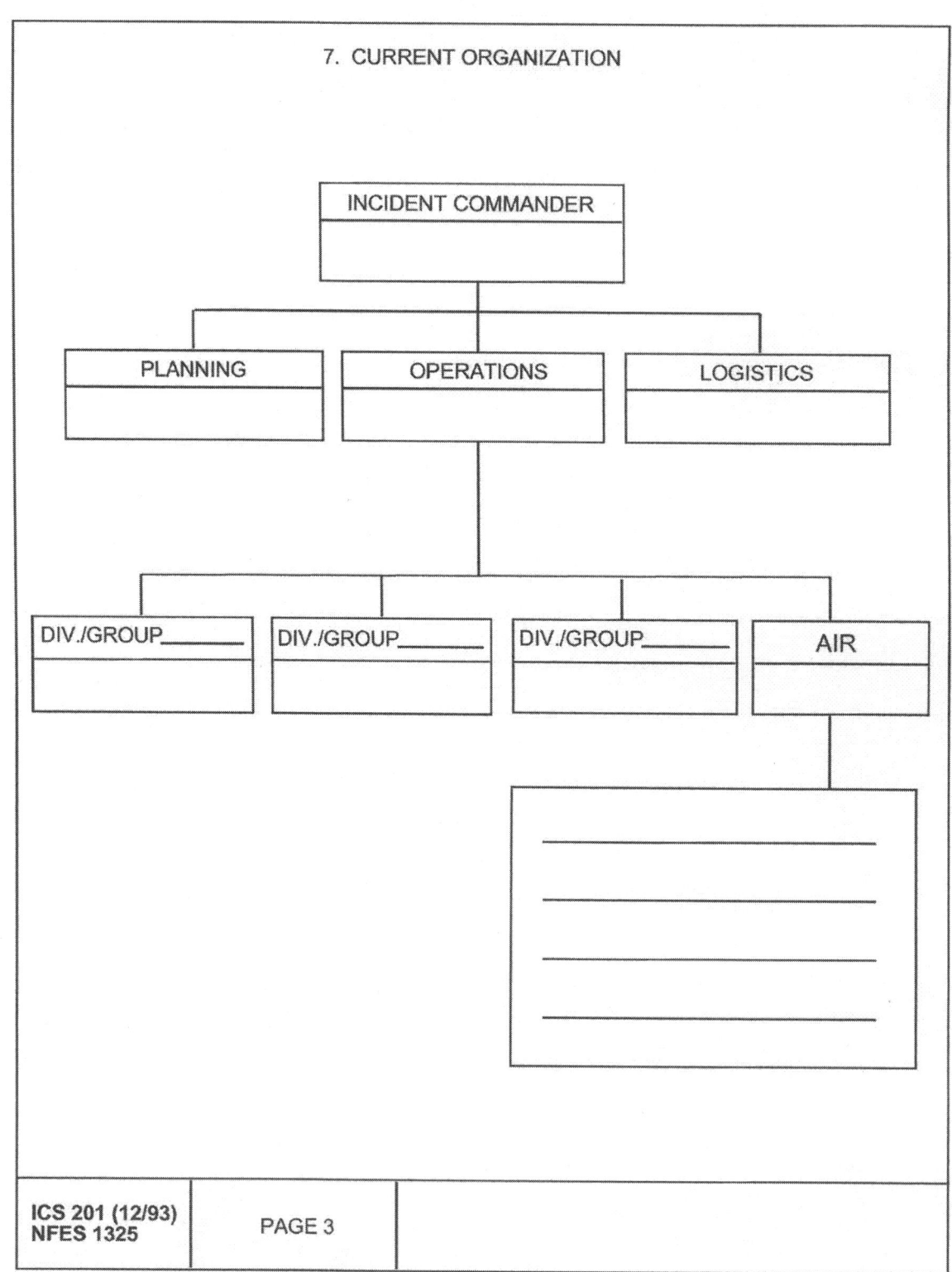

8. RESOURCES SUMMARY					
RESOURCES ORDERED	RESOURCES IDENTIFICATION	ETA	ON SCENE √	LOCATION/ASSIGNMENT

ICS 201 (12/93)
NFES 1325   PAGE 4

Appendix 2 - Incident Command System Assignment List 204 Form

ASSIGNMENT LIST

1. BRANCH
2. DIVISION/GROUP
3. INCIDENT NAME
4. OPERATIONAL PERIOD
   DATE _____ TIME _____

5. OPERATIONAL PERSONNEL

OPERATIONS CHIEF _____ DIVISION/GROUP SUPERVISOR _____

BRANCH DIRECTOR _____ AIR TACTICAL GROUP SUPERVISOR _____

6. RESOURCES ASSIGNED THIS PERIOD

STRIKE TEAM/TASK FORCE/ RESOURCE DESIGNATOR	EMT	LEADER	NUMBER PERSONS	TRANS. NEEDED	PICKUP PT./TIME	DROP OFF PT./TIME

7. CONTROL OPERATIONS

8. SPECIAL INSTRUCTIONS

9. DIVISION/GROUP COMMUNICATIONS SUMMARY

FUNCTION		FREQ.	SYSTEM	CHAN.	FUNCTION		FREQ.	SYSTEM	CHAN.
COMMAND	LOCAL				SUPPORT	LOCAL			
	REPEAT					REPEAT			
DIV./GROUP TACTICAL					GROUND TO AIR				

PREPARED BY (RESOURCE UNIT LEADER)	APPROVED BY (PLANNING SECT. CH.)	DATE	TIME

204 ICS (1/99) NFES 1328

Appendix 3 - Incident Command System Medical Plan 206 Form

MEDICAL PLAN	1. INCIDENT NAME	2. DATE PREPARED	3. TIME PREPARED	4. OPERATIONAL PERIOD

5. INCIDENT MEDICAL AID STATIONS

MEDICAL AID STATIONS	LOCATION	PARAMEDICS	
		YES	NO

6. TRANSPORTATION

A. AMBULANCE SERVICES

NAME	ADDRESS	PHONE	PARAMEDICS	
			YES	NO

B. INCIDENT AMBULANCES

NAME	LOCATION	PARAMEDICS	
		YES	NO

7. HOSPITALS

NAME	ADDRESS	TRAVEL TIME		PHONE	HELIPAD		BURN CENTER	
		AIR	GRND		YES	NO	YES	NO

8. MEDICAL EMERGENCY PROCEDURES

206 ICS 8/78	9. PREPARED BY (MEDICAL UNIT LEADER) 10. REVIEWED BY (SAFETY OFFICER)

NFES 1331

Appendix 4 - Incident Command System Check-In 211 Form

Appendix 5 - Incident Search Urgency Form

SEARCH URGENCY FORM

Remember The Lower The Number The More Urgent The Response

RATING

A) NUMBER OF SUBJECTS
- One Person 1
- Two Person (if still together) 2
- Three Person (if still together) 3

B) AGE
- Very Young (10 yrs and under) 1
- Very Old (75 yrs or older) 1
- Other 2-4

C) MEDICAL CONDITION
- Known illness requiring medication 1
- Known or suspected injury or illness 2
- Healthy 3
- Known Fatality 4

D) PHYSICAL CONDITION
- Unfit 1
- Fit 2
- Very Fit 3

E) CLOTHING PROFILE
- Inadequate or insufficient for environment 1
- Adequate for environment 2
- Very Good 3

F) EQUIPMENT PROFILE
- Inadequate for activity/environment 1
- Questionable for environment 2
- Adequate for environment 3
- Very Well Equipped 4

G) SUBJECT EXPERIENCE PROFILE
- Not experienced, not familiar with the area 1
- Not experienced, knows the area 2
- Experienced, not familiar with the area 3
- Experienced, knows the area 4

H) WEATHER PROFILE
- Existing hazardous weather 1
- Predicted hazardous weather (8 hrs. or less) 2
- Predicted hazardous weather (more than 8 hrs.) 3
- No hazardous weather predicted 4

I) TERRAIN & HAZARDS PROFILE
- Known hazardous terrain or other hazards 1
- Difficult terrain 2
- Few hazards 3
- Easy terrain, no known hazards 4

TOTAL:

IF ANY OF THE NINE CATEGORIES ARE RATED AS A ONE (1), REGARDLESS OF THE TOTAL, THE SEARCH MAY REQUIRE AN *EMERGENCY RESPONSE*.

The total should range from 9 to 33, with 9 being the most URGENT!

9-17 Emergency Response   18-27 Measured Response   28-33 Evaluate & Investigate

Appendix 6 - Lost Person Questionnaire Form

LOST PERSON QUESTIONNAIRE

NOTE: Use pencil/black ink, print clearly, avoid confusing phrases/words, unfamiliar abbreviations. Complete and detail answers for future use. Answer ALL questions, if possible.

INCIDENT TITLE: _____ TODAY'S DATE: _____ TIME: _____

Officer Taking Info: _____ Incident #:SAR #: _____

A. SOURCE(S) OF INFORMATION FOR QUESTIONNAIRE

Name: How taken (phone,etc.) _____
Home Address: Zip: _____
Phone #: (___) _____ 2nd phone #: (___) _____ Relationship: _____

Where/how to contact now: _____
Where/how to contact later: _____
What does informant believe happened? _____

B. LOST PERSON

Full Name: _____ Sex: _M_ _F_ Nicknames: _____

Home Address: _____ Zip: _____

Local Address: _____ Zip: _____

Home Phone #: (___) _____ Local phone #: (___) _____

D.O.B.: _____ Birthplace: _____

C. PHYSICAL DESCRIPTION

Height: _____ Weight: _____ Age: _____ Build: _____ Eye Color: _____

Hair: Color: _____ Length: _____ Style: _____

    Beard: _____ Mustache: _____ Sideburns: _____

Facial features/shape: _____ Complexion: _____

Distinguishing marks (scars, moles): _____

Overall appearance: _____

Photo available?_Y N_ Where: _____ Need to be returned?_Y N_

Comments: _____
_____
_____

D. TRIP PLANS OF SUBJECT

Started from: _____ Day/Date: _____ Time: _____

Going to: _____ Via: _____

Purpose: _____

For how long? _____ Exit date: _____ Alone? _Y_ _N_ Group Size: _____

Done trip before? _Y_ _N_ Details: _____

Transported by whom/means: _____

Vehicle now located at: _____ Type: _____ Color: _____

   License # _____ State: _____ Verified? _Y_ _N_ By Whom: _____

Return time: _____ From where: _____

   By whom/what: _____

Additional names, cars, licenses, etc. for party: _____

Alternate plans/routes/objectives discussed: _____

   Discussed with whom: _____ When: _____

Comments: _____
_____
_____

E. CLOTHING

	Style	Color	Size	Other

Shirt/sweater: _____

Pants: _____

Outer wear: _____

Inner wear: _____

Head wear: _____

Rain wear: _____

Glasses: _____

Gloves: _____

Extra clothing: _____

Footwear: _____

   sole type: _____ sample available? _Y_ _N_ where: _____

Scent articles available? __Y__ __N__ What _____ Secured? __Y__ __N__

Where is the scent article now? _____

Overall coloration as seen from air: _____

F. LAST SEEN

Time: _____ Where: _____ Why/how: _____

Seen by whom: _____ Location now: _____

Who last talked at length with person: _____

  where: _____ Subject matter: _____

Weather at time: _____ Weather since: _____

Seen going which way: _____ When: _____

Reason for leaving: _____

Attitude (confident, confused, etc.): _____

Subject complaining of anything: _____

Subject seem tired: _____ Cold/hot: _____ Other: _____

COMMENTS: _____

_____

G. OUTDOOR EXPERIENCE

Familiar with area:? __Y__ __N__ How recent: _____ Other: _____

Other areas of travel: _____

Formal outdoor training degree: _____

  Where: _____ When: _____

Medical training: _____ When: _____

Scouting experience: _____ When: _____ Where: _____

  How much: _____ Scout rank: _____ Scout Leader? __Y__ __N__

Military experience? __Y__ __N__ What: _____ When: _____ Where: _____

  Rank: _____ Other: _____

Generalized previous experience: _____

How much overnight experience: _____

Ever been lost before? __Y__ __N__ Where: _____ When: _____

Ever go out alone? __Y__ __N__ Where: _____

Stay on trails or X-C: _____

Now fast does subject hike: _____

Athletic/other interests: _____

Climbing experience: _____

COMMENTS: _____

H. HABITS/PERSONALITY

Smoke? __Y__ __N__ How often: _____ What: _____ Brand: _____

Alcohol? __Y__ __N__ How often: _____ What: _____ Brand: _____

Recreational drugs? __Y__ __N__ How often: _____ What: _____

Gum Brand: _____ Candy Brand: _____ Other: _____

Hobbies/Interests: _____

Outgoing/quiet: _____ Gregarious/loner: _____

Evidence of leadership: _____ Give up easy/Keep Going: _____

Legal trouble (past/present): _____

Hitchhike? __Y__ __N__ Accepts rides easily: _____

Personal Problems: _____

Religious? __Y__ __N__ Faith: _____ To What Degree: _____

Personal values: _____

Philosophy: _____

Person closest to: _____ In family: _____

Emotional history: _____

Education: Highest Grade Achieved: _____ Current status: _____ College Education: _____

    School name: _____

    Teacher(s): _____

    Subject/degree: _____ Year: _____

Local/fictional hero: _____

COMMENTS: _____

I. HEALTH/GENERAL CONDITION

Overall health: _____

Overall physical condition: _____

Known medical/dental problems: _____

    Knowledgeable doctor: _____ Phone # (___) _____

Handicaps: _____

Known psychological problems: _____

    Knowledgeable person: _____ Phone # (___) _____

Medication: _____ Dosages: _____

    Knowledgeable person: _____ Phone # (___) _____

    What will happen without meds.: _____

Eyesight without glasses: _____ Spares? _Y_ _N_ Where are spares: _____

    COMMENTS: _____

_____

J. EQUIPMENT

	Style	Color	Brand	Size
Pack:				
Tent:				
Sleeping bag:				
Ground cloth/pad				
Fishing equipment:				
Climbing equipment:				
Light:				
Knife:				
Camera:				
Stove:	Fuel:		Fire starter? Y N What:	
Liquid container:		How much fluid:	What kind fluid:	
Compass:		Map:	Of where:	
How competent with map/compass:				

Food: _____ Brands: _____

_____

Skiis: Type:_____ Brand: _____ Color: _____ Size:_____

   Bindings:_____ Pole type: _____ Length: _____

   How competent: _____

Snowshoes: Type:_____ Brand: _____ Color: _____ Size: _____

   Bindings: _____ How competent: _____

Firearms? _Y_ _N_ Brand: _____ Model: _____ Holster:_____

Money: Amount:_____ Credit Cards: _____

Other documents: _____

COMMENTS: _____

_____

K. CONTACTS PERSON WOULD MAKE UPON REACHING CIVILIZATION

Full Name: _____ Relationship: _____

Address: _____ Zip: _____

Phone #: (____) _____ Anyone home now: _____

L. CHILDREN

Afraid of dark?_Y_ _N_ Animals? _Y_ _N_ Afraid of: _____

Feeling toward adults: _____ Strangers:_____

Reactions when hurt: _____ Cry: _____

Training when lost: _____

Active/lethargic/antisocial: _____

COMMENTS:_____

_____

M. GROUPS OVERDUE

Name/kind of group: _____ Leader:_____

Experience of group/leader: _____

Address/phone of knowledgeable person: _____

Personality clashes within group: _____

Leader types in group other than leader: _____

What would subject do if separated from group: _____

Competitive spirit of group: _____

Intragroup dynamics: _____

COMMENTS: _____
_____

N. ACTIONS TAKEN SO FAR

By: Family/friends: _____ Results: _____
_____

Others: _____ Results: _____

COMMENTS: _____
_____

O. PRESS/FAMILY RELATIONS

Next of kin: _____ Relationship: _____

Address: _____ Zip: _____

Phone #: (____) _____ Occupation: _____

Person to notify when subject found: _____ Relationship: _____

Address: _____ Zip: _____

Phone #: (____) _____ Occupation: _____

Significant family problems: _____

Family's desire to employ special assistance: _____

COMMENTS: _____
_____

P. OTHER INFORMATION

_____
_____
_____

Appendix 7 - Incident Command System 214 Form – Unit Log

UNIT LOG	1. Incident Name	2. Date Prepared	3. Time Prepared
4. Unit Name/Designators	5. Unit Leader (Name and Position)		6. Operational Period

7. Personnel Roster Assigned		
Name	ICS Position	Home Base

8. Activity Log	
Time	Major Events

9. Prepared by (Name and Position)

ICS 214

Illustrations, Photographs credit

Photograph Credits -

Alaska Mountain Rescue Group
Air Force Personnel Center, Randolph AFB, Texas
Brunton Compass
City of Bethlehem Water Rescue Team, Bethlehem PA
City of Orlando Fire Department, FL
Civil Air Patrol
Coconino County Sheriff Department, Coconino AZ
Federal Emergency Management Agency -NIMS
Fire Department of New York, NYC
Jim Barlett; www.jwbartlett.com
K-9 Alert Search & Rescue Dogs, Inc.
Maryland State Police, MD
Over the Edge, Inc., Piscataway NJ
Port Richmond C.E.R.T., Staten Island NY
Passaic County Sheriff's Department, Wayne NJ
South Old Bridge Fire Department, South Old Bridge NJ
White Deer Search & Rescue, Columbia PA
www.absarokasearchdogs.org/our_teams/crystal_arnold.php
www.bigmtnbelgians.com/
www.vetmed.ucdavis.edu

Illustrations –

Cole Brown, III
Eric H. Martin

Cover –
Designed by
Design Consultants, Inc.
2306 Lookout Rd.
Haymarket, VA 20169

Cover photographs provided by:
City of Bethlehem Water Rescue Team, Bethlehem PA
Coconino County Sheriff's Department, AZ
Maryland State Police, MD
Maine Search & Rescue Dogs, ME
Orlando Fire Department, FL
Over the Edge, Inc., NJ
Passaic County Sheriff's Department, Wayne NJ
Port Richmond C.E.R.T., NY
South Old Bridge Fire Department, NJ

Made in the USA
Middletown, DE
10 March 2021